Bedside Manners

A Comedy

Derek Benfield

Samuel French – London
New York – Sydney – Toronto – Hollywood

BEDSIDE MANNERS

First presented at the Contra-Kreis Theater, Bonn, on 4th December 1986, with the following cast of characters:

Roger	Claus Tinney
Ferris	Gerd Neubert
Geoff	Christian Ebel
Sally	Christine Mederer
Helen	Sylvia Nentwig

Translated and directed by Horst Johanning
Setting by Pit Fischer

Subsequently presented by Trent Theatre Productions on a National Tour which opened at the Playhouse, Salisbury, on 16th March 1989, with the following cast of characters:

Roger	Maurice Thorogood
Ferris	John Inman
Geoff	Peter Symonds
Sally	Nikki Kelly
Helen	Georgina Moon

The play directed by Bill Roberton
Setting by Bill Crutcher

The play takes place in a small, unfashionable hotel somewhere in the depths of the country.

ACT I   Early evening on a Friday in the Spring
ACT II   A few moments later

Time—the present

Also by Derek Benfield:

Flying Feathers
Touch and Go
Look Who's Talking!
Beyond a Joke
Caught on the Hop
Fish Out of Water
In For the Kill
Panic Stations
A Bird in the Hand
Murder for the Asking
Off the Hook!
Post Horn Gallop
Running Riot
Wild Goose Chase

ACT I

A small unfashionable hotel in the depths of the country

A modest entrance hall with a reception desk, beyond which is a swing door leading to the kitchen and the first few steps of two staircases, one leading up and off to the L and the other up and off to the R. There is a way off to the restaurant DL and to the main entrance DR. There is a drinks trolley and a low chair on one side of the reception area and a small sofa and table on the other. There are two identical bedrooms: one R, decorated green, the other L, decorated blue. These are raised about a foot above the level of the reception area. Each bedroom has a door to the corridor, another to the bathroom, a bed, a chair and a table on which is a telephone. The lighting in the reception area will remain on throughout, whereas the lights in the bedrooms will come on and off as required. Theme music (preferably "There's a Small Hotel") before the play will continue after the curtain rises until the dialogue starts

The Lights come up in the Green Room. Roger is lying on the bed. He is an attractive, assured young man. After a moment, his arm comes up over his head and he looks at his wristwatch. He gets up, straightens his tie and shirt, and looks at the bed. He tests its springiness with his hands and smiles, approvingly. Then, humming along with the music, he goes into the bathroom. He returns with a toothbrush and a glass of water, brushing his teeth noisily. He glances again at his wristwatch (the toothbrush hand) and goes back into the bathroom. We hear him gargling. He returns with an eau de cologne spray and anoints his face liberally. It stings a bit. He notices his shoes by the bed, goes across and gives a short, sharp spray into each one. He puts down the eau de cologne and tidies his hair. Then, satisfied with his fatal attraction, he lifts the telephone receiver. It is out of order. He rattles the rest and tries again. Nothing. He replaces the receiver, puts on his shoes and jacket and goes out into the corridor, closing the door behind him

Roger comes down the R stairs into the reception area. Seeing nobody about he goes to the desk and bangs on the bell. He waits. Nothing

Roger (*calling impatiently*) Ferris! Ferris!
Ferris (*off*) All right! All right! I'm coming. There's no need to shout.

Ferris comes in through the swing doors. He is an unenthusiastic man in his 40s. He is eating a sandwich and carrying a copy of the 'Daily Mirror'. He sees Roger

Oh, it's you. I might have guessed.
Roger It's not working!
Ferris Didn't *sound* as if it wasn't working. (*He peers at the bell*)

Roger Not the bell! Up there. In my bedroom. It's not working in my bedroom.

Ferris Oh, dear. What a shame ... (*He chuckles*)

Roger Well? What are you going to do about it?

Ferris There's nothing *I* can do. If you've got a personal problem, you'd better see a doctor. (*He munches his sandwich and peruses his paper*)

Roger (*glaring at him*) There nothing wrong with *my* equipment! It's the telephone.

Ferris What?

Roger Telephone!

Ferris Oh. Over there.

Roger No, no—the telephone in my room! It's not working.

Ferris You want to talk to somebody?

Roger Yes! I want to talk to *you*!

Ferris Well, I'm here. There's no need to telephone.

Roger You mean every time I want to speak to you I have to come traipsing down here?

Ferris (*considering*) Well ... I suppose you *could* bang three times on the floor.

Roger What if I want something in the middle of the night? I can't go banging about on the floor in the middle of the night.

Ferris Well, that's up to you, isn't it?

Roger You'll have to get it mended!

Ferris I can't do that. Not until Monday.

Roger (*looking at him in despair*) But what about room service?

Ferris Well, there won't *be* any, will there? Not for *you*, anyway. Will you be wanting something, then?

Roger (*impatiently*) Well—you never know! A cup of hot chocolate. Cheese on toast. ...

Ferris (*helpfully*) Well, I tell you what. We'll work out a code, eh? How about that? Three bangs for hot chocolate. Two for cheese on toast.

Roger (*smiling secretly*) What about ... champagne?

Ferris Oh, you'll have to bang away like mad for champagne! Who are you expecting, then—the Princess of Wales?

Roger Not exactly, no.

Ferris Oh, she *will* be disappointed. Well, if I hear you banging away on the floor I'll bring up the bubbly.

Roger Was it so obvious?

Ferris What?

Roger That I was expecting somebody.

Ferris Well—ponging of after-shave and talking about champagne doesn't sound to me like a business appointment.

Roger Ah. No. Quite.

Ferris chuckles and leans forward confidentially, his mouth full of sandwich

Ferris Not your wife, though, is it?

Roger (*defensively*) How do *you* know?

Ferris Well ... champagne in the middle of the night ... ?

Roger (*anxious to get on*) Anyway, if a young lady arrives, send her up to me. All right?

Ferris Any particular young lady, or the first female through the front door?

Roger (*romantically*) Very pretty . . .

Ferris I'll see what I can do, sir. (*He starts to go*)

Roger No, no, you fool! *My* young lady! She's very pretty. She'll ask for Mr Smith. And when she does—send her up.

Ferris Mr Smith. Send her up. Very good, sir. (*He holds out his hand, pointedly*)

Roger Oh—yes. (*He gives Ferris a coin and goes out up the* R *stairs*)

Ferris (*assuming surprise*) Oh, thank you, Mr Smith! Very nice of you to think of it, sir.

Music up as Ferris pockets the money, gratefully, goes to lean on his desk and studies the 'Daily Mirror', eating his sandwich. The music continues until the dialogue starts again

Roger comes into the Green Room. He sits on the end of the bed, sighs happily, and lies back again to wait

Lights crossfade from Green Room to Blue Room

Geoff is lying on the bed. After a moment, his arm comes up over his head and he looks at his wristwatch. He stands up on the bed and does a few exercises. Unlike Roger, he is rather unsure of himself, a small man with an appealing innocence. He goes into the bathroom. He returns with a toothbrush and a glass of water, brushing his teeth, noisily. He glances at his watch again, but it is the hand that holds the glass so he spills some of the water onto the floor. In panic, he hastily rubs it into the carpet with his stocking foot and hastens back into the bathroom. We hear him gargling. He returns with an eau de cologne spray. He holds it, uncertainly, closes his eyes and sprays, but misses his face completely. He realizes his error and pursues the cloud of eau de cologne with his face. He puts down the spray and tidies his hair. Not too confident about his fatal attraction, he goes to the telephone and lifts the receiver. It is out of order. He rattles the rest and tries again. Nothing. He replaces the receiver, puts on his shoes, and goes out into the corridor, closing the door behind him. Geoff comes down the L *stairs into the reception area. He goes to the desk and looks, hopefully, at the back of the 'Daily Mirror'. He clears his throat. No reaction from Ferris. Geoff looks at the bell on the desk, hesitates, then plucks up courage and hits it. But rather gently. It emits a small ting*

Ferris lowers his newspaper, abruptly, and peers at the bell and then at Geoff, belligerently

Ferris What do *you* want?

Geoff (*taken aback*) Sorry?

Ferris Don't tell me *yours* isn't working either.

Geoff Sorry?

Ferris The telephone! In your bedroom.

Geoff Oh. No. It isn't.

Ferris (*darkly*) Have you been fiddling with it?
Geoff No!

Glaring at him, Ferris folds up his newspaper, puts it down and leans on the desk to get a closer look at Geoff

Ferris Are you up to something?
Geoff What?
Ferris Well, you seem in a bit of a state.
Geoff (*giving a small nervous laugh*) I expect my watch is fast. Has—has anyone been looking for me?
Ferris How do *I* know?
Geoff Well, I—I thought—as you *work* here. . . .
Ferris You don't think I'd work in a place like this, do you? I'm just filling in while my sister's on holiday.
Geoff Oh. I see. But—as far as you know—nobody's . . . ?
Ferris Frinton. You ever been there?
Geoff (*puzzled*) What?
Ferris Frinton. That's where my sister's gone.
Geoff Oh. No.
Ferris She thought of Benidorm.
Geoff Really?
Ferris Oh, yes. Decided on Frinton, though. Expecting someone, then, are you?
Geoff Yes. (*Embarrassed*) I'm expecting a lady . . .
Ferris Expecting a baby?
Geoff A lady!
Ferris Oh. Well, if I hear you banging about on the floor I'll bring up the bubbly.
Geoff I beg your pardon?
Ferris Oh, no. That was the other one, wasn't it?
Geoff What other one?
Ferris Never mind. No champagne for you, then?
Geoff Well, I . . . I hadn't thought about it.
Ferris I'd better make a note of that in case I forget. We don't want to get confused, do we? (*He writes on a pad*) No champagne in Blue. . . . Right you are, sir. If you need any help I'll be down here.
Geoff What?
Ferris In case you fancy anything in the middle of the night.
Geoff Sorry?
Ferris (*impatiently*) Well—you never know! Hot chocolate. Cheese on toast. . . .
Geoff Oh. Right. Thanks. (*He starts to go*)
Ferris Haven't you forgotten something?

Geoff stops

Geoff Have I?
Ferris (*wearily*) How shall I know which one's for you, sir?
Geoff (*blankly*) What?
Ferris Well, for all I know, there may be hordes of young ladies arriving

tonight. How am I to know which is the lucky one who's destined to end up in Blue—with you—and no champagne?

Geoff (*smiling, self-consciously*) Very pretty. . . . She'll ask for Mr Smith.

Ferris Mr Smith. (*He reacts*) Mr Smith!

Geoff Yes. And when she does—send her up.

Ferris Send her up. Very good, sir. (*He holds out his hand, rather pointedly*)

Geoff Oh—thanks very much! (*He shakes Ferris by the hand and goes out up the L stairs*)

Ferris starts to go, muttering

Ferris Thank you, Mr Smith. Very kind of you, sir. Nice of you to think of it, I'm sure.

The music comes in as Ferris disappears through the swing door and continues until the dialogue starts again

Geoff comes into the Blue Room. He sits on the end of the bed, tries to look confident like Roger did, but fails. He lies back on the bed to wait. Lights out in Blue Room

Sally comes in from the main entrance. She is extremely attractive and carries a weekend case. She goes to the desk, looking about, obviously seeing it all for the first time. She sees the bell and hits it

Ferris comes in through the swing door from the kitchen, none too hastily, a glass of beer in his hand

The music fades

(*Grumbling*) Honestly, I'm run off my feet in this place. . . . (*He sips his beer*)

Sally (*looking about*) It doesn't *look* very busy.

Ferris I'll be the judge of that. What can I do for you?

She smiles happily, and holds up her weekend case to show him

Sally I'm coming to stay here!

He peers at the case, unimpressed

Ferris Oh, yes?

Sally Well, I am expected.

He sniffs, unconvinced, and goes behind the reception desk. He puts down his beer and picks up the hotel register. He gives her a suspicious look

Ferris Right. Let's see if we can find you in here, then, shall we?

He opens the register, but she closes it abruptly. It emits a cloud of dust. They both choke a little

Now, what did you go and do that for?

Sally Well you won't find me in there.

Ferris You said you were expected.

Sally Yes, but I haven't got a booking. (*She leans forward; confidentially*) I'm looking for a man.

Ferris Well, you've come to the right place. We've got two spare ones upstairs!

Sally (*laughing*) Not *any* man!

Ferris Oh. A special man?

Sally Of course a special man. (*Embarrassed*) A ... a Mr Smith. I'm meeting him here.

Ferris Ah! So you're one of *them*!

Sally (*puzzled*) Sorry?

Ferris You're in luck.

Sally Am I?

Ferris Oh, yes. You're the first.

Sally (*surprised*) You mean he's expecting more than one?

Ferris (*laughing*) No, no! They're expecting one each. (*He smiles, cosily*) Now which one do *you* want?

Sally Do I have a choice?

Ferris Well, there are two Mr Smiths. One in Blue and one in Green, and they're both expecting.

Sally (*puzzled*) Blue? Green?

Ferris The rooms are named after the colours of the walls.

Sally Oh, I see. And there's one in each?

Ferris Oh, yes. And they're both up there now—waiting.

Sally drifts away a little, rather put out

Sally I would have thought it would have been more polite to wait down here. ...

He comes out from behind the desk and follows her

Ferris Exactly what I thought! But perhaps they were tired. Felt in need of a sleep.

Sally At this time? They'll be sleeping tonight.

Ferris Oh. Perhaps they hadn't realized that. Right—which one do *you* want, then?

Sally (*humouring him*) Well, what do they look like?

Ferris One's tall and dark, and the other's not so tall and fair.

Sally I ... think I'll try the tall dark one.

Ferris (*smiling*) Ah! You've chosen well.

Sally Have I?

Ferris Oh, yes. This is your lucky day.

Sally (*smiling*) I'm very glad to hear it.

Ferris You're getting the champagne.

Sally (*delighted*) Champagne? Really?

Ferris Yes. As soon as you start banging on the floor.

Sally (*looking a little surprised*) I beg your pardon?

Ferris That's what we arranged.

Sally We?

Ferris Your Mr Smith and me.

Sally (*a little annoyed*) You arranged it together?

Ferris Yes, of course. We've worked out a code, see? So I always know what he wants in the middle of the night.

Sally (*doubtfully*) I see ...

Ferris So the minute I hear you banging on the floor, I'll be in through the door with the bubbly. Mind you, if it's only a couple of *small* bangs you'll have to settle for hot chocolate.

Sally And which room do I want, then? For *my* Mr Smith.

Ferris Oh—Green. You want the green Mr Smith. Through the arch and up the stairs to the left. You can't miss it.

Sally Thank you.

Ferris Shall I help you with your bag, miss?

Sally (*with a smile*) It's all right. I think I can manage.

She goes out through the arch and up the R *stairs. He looks after her retreating legs*

Ferris (*as she goes*) Yes. I bet you can. I wish my watch had got a movement like that ...

He goes out through the swing door into the kitchen

Lights up in Green Room. A knock on the door. Roger sits up, abruptly. He gets off the bed, tidies his hair and goes, optimistically, to the door. He opens it and gazes at Sally, delightedly. He holds out his arms to be embraced but she walks past him into the room. He looks surprised, closes the door and follows her. She puts down her weekend case on the armchair

Sally So this is where you are!

Roger Yes. I was having a lie-down.

Sally So I heard.

Roger What?

Sally From the man downstairs.

Roger Ferris.

Sally What?

Roger That's his name.

Sally Well, he said you'd be up here.

Roger Yes. I was. I was waiting for you.

Sally I wasn't late.

Roger I didn't say you were, darling.

Sally Though it wouldn't have been surprising if I had been. Did you have to choose such an isolated place? I should think they deliver the post by carrier pigeon.

Roger Well, we've got to be discreet. We don't want all our friends wandering in, do we?

Sally (*glancing around the room*) There wouldn't be much room for them, would there?

Roger I saw this place advertised in the parish magazine.

Sally Don't say we're going to come face-to-face with the Archbishop of Canterbury.

Roger It said, "Escape from it all to peace and tranquillity".

Sally Well, it's certainly tranquil. Getting here was like taking an Army survival course. I had to stop and buy a compass.

Roger Well, we've got each other, darling. Just think of it—two whole days all on our own!

Sally Yes. . . .

They kiss, and enjoy it. He starts to guide them both gently on to the bed, but she restrains him

Where are we going?

Roger I thought it would be more comfortable on here. Why? What's the matter?

Sally I haven't unpacked yet.

Roger Well, that won't take you very long.

He tries again, but again she holds back

Sally Darling, there's no hurry.

Roger Isn't there?

Sally Of course not.

Roger Oh. I didn't know that.

Sally You said yourself we've got two whole days. You don't have to keep going all the time. You're not entering the marathon.

Ferris comes through the swing doors from the kitchen, carrying a screwdriver. He goes up the R stairs

Sally drifts away from Roger, a little hurt

I thought you'd have waited for me downstairs. I was so embarrassed down there on my own. I felt like a loose woman.

Roger You *are* a loose woman.

Sally Well, I don't want to *look* like one, do I?

Roger I'm sorry, darling. I was getting everything ready for you up here.

Sally You were lying down!

Roger Yes. And everything was ready for you.

Sally (*sulking a little*) You never said I'd be sharing a green room with a man named Smith. . . .

Roger I told you. We have to be discreet.

Sally Couldn't you have called yourself Popkiss or something?

Roger Popkiss?

Sally Well, *every*body calls themselves Smith.

Roger Do they?

Sally Of course they do. Anyone who's up to no good. There are two of you in this hotel already.

Roger Really? You were lucky to get the right one, then, weren't you?

They smile and go into a kiss, sinking on to the bed

Whereupon, the door opens and Ferris walks in, closing it behind him with a bang.

Roger and Sally leap apart, embarrassed. He goes to Ferris angrily

How dare you come barging in here like that!

Ferris Well, you hadn't locked the door. If you're up to no good before nightfall you ought to lock the door. The chambermaid will want to turn the bed down.

Roger She doesn't have to bother! We can do it ourselves.

Ferris Yes. I'm sure you can! (*He crosses to Sally; chattily*) You found him all right, then, miss?

Sally Yes, thank you.

Ferris Was the right one, was it?

Sally I'll let you know in the morning.

Ferris and Sally laugh at her little joke. Roger does not. He glares at Ferris

Roger What the hell do you want?

Ferris I came to see to the telephone.

Roger Not now!

Ferris But I've brought my screwdriver. (*He holds up his screwdriver*)

Roger You're not doing it now!

Ferris Neither should you be! I thought you'd be having food first. (*He goes to examine the telephone*)

Roger (*vehementlyly*) We don't want you in here now! You said it couldn't be fixed till Monday!

Ferris (*equally vehement*) And *you* said you were worried about room service! So I thought I'd have a little tinker with it myself! (*He unscrews the mouthpiece to look inside*)

Roger You can have a little tinker with it later!

Ferris Oh, no. I don't want to disturb you later. (*He screws up the mouthpiece again*)

Roger You *have* disturbed us!

Ferris Would you like me to unpack your bag, miss?

Roger No, she wouldn't!

Ferris Anything you say, sir. I'll leave you to it, then. (*He starts to go, then turns back again*) Oh, by the way—

Roger (*seething*) Now what?

Ferris I've put "you-know-what" on ice, ready for later on. But I'll wait till I hear you on the floor.

He winks, saucily, and goes, closing the door behind him

Roger I can't stand that man.

Sally I think he's rather nice.

Roger You would!

Sally Oh, darling—don't be cross. We've only got two days . . . (*She gets up and puts her arms around him*)

Roger Good lord, so we have!

They embrace, hurriedly.

Ferris re-appears. They leap apart

Ferris Shall I make that *two* bottles of "you-know-what"?

Roger Get out!

Ferris That's what I thought you'd say.

He goes again, closing the door. Roger and Sally resume their embrace

Sally You know ... this is going to be a new experience for me.
Roger Sorry?
Sally Well ... I've never done this before.
Roger Done what?
Sally Slept with a married man.
Roger (*appalled*) I never told you I was married!
Sally (*with a smile*) You didn't have to.
Roger (*gloomily*) Good lord. Is it *so* obvious?

She moves away from him, collects her weekend case and goes towards the bathroom

Where are you going?
Sally To have a bath and change for dinner.
Roger Dinner?
Sally We are going to *eat*, aren't we?
Roger (*who had not thought of it*) Oh—yes. Yes, I suppose so.

Sally smiles, and goes out to the bathroom

Roger sighs and lies down on the bed to wait, patiently. Lights out in Green Room. Music up until the dialogue starts

Helen comes in from the main entrance. She is a nice-looking girl, if not exactly glamorous, and has a tendency to be rather clumsy. Somewhat incongruously, she is wearing sun-glasses. She carries a weekend case, a handbag and a box of chocolates. She looks about, apprehensively, crossing to the reception desk

Unseen by her, Ferris returns and watches her. She sees the bell, edges gradually to it, plucks up courage—and hits it so hard that it falls to the floor! She picks it up, quickly

Ferris And what do you think *you're* doing?
Helen (*jumping nervously*) Aah!

He ambles across to her, critically

Ferris You can't go around knocking people's bells off like that. (*He takes the bell from her and puts it back in its accustomed place*)
Helen I—I'm sorry. It was an accident. I'll try not to do it again.
Ferris Perhaps you couldn't see where you were going?
Helen What?

He indicates her sun-glasses. She holds onto them nervously

Ferris I should take them off, if I were you. You're not in Benidorm, you know.

She reacts with delight, surprised by his apparent intuition

Helen We *thought* of Benidorm!
Ferris (*blankly*) What?

Helen We thought of Benidorm ...
Ferris Who did?
Helen *We* did!
Ferris You didn't!
Helen We did! Before deciding on this place.
Ferris So did my sister.
Helen Really?
Ferris Yes. Before she went to Frinton.
Helen I read about it in the parish magazine.
Ferris (*astonished*) About Frinton?
Helen About *this* place.
Ferris Oh. But by then I suppose you'd already bought your sun-glasses?
Helen Yes ...
Ferris Well, never mind, eh? You might go to Benidorm *next* year.

Helen turns and knocks something else off the reception desk. He just manages to catch it, like an expert slip-fielder

Ferris (*patiently*) Look—you'd better take 'em off before you do any damage.

She holds on to her sun-glasses, protectively

Helen Oh, no! No! I can't do that!
Ferris Why not? They do *come* off, don't they?
Helen I don't want anyone to recognize me.
Ferris Why not? (*Then, intrigued*) Here—are you a film star? (*He pushes her, playfully*)

She smiles, flattered

Helen No, of course not, silly. ... (*She looks about, furtively*) I'm—I'm supposed to meet someone here.
Ferris (*grinning, delightedly*) Mr Smith!
Helen Aah! (*She jumps a mile and drops her box of chocolates*)

Ferris goes to help her, but she collides with him as they bend down at the same time. He looks at her patiently

Ferris Look, miss—you just stay there, eh? *I'll* pick them up. I'm just filling in here, you see? And I don't want to have a fatal accident. Not before my sister gets back from Frinton. (*He picks up the box of chocolates and hands it back to her*)
Helen Thank you.
Ferris So—you're the other one for Mr Smith, then?
Helen (*puzzled*) What other one?
Ferris (*sighing, regretfully*) Pity you weren't here sooner.
Helen Why?
Ferris You could have had first choice.
Helen I beg your pardon?
Ferris But now—well, you're in Blue, and *he* says no champagne.
Helen No champagne?

Ferris I'm afraid not. I've got a note of it over here.

He jumps up neatly and lands on his stomach on top of the desk to reach over and get the note

There we are, see? "No champagne in Blue". I think it's outrageous. Nice little thing like you. Bit of a skinflint, is he? Your Mr Smith.

Helen I don't think so. . . .

Ferris Well, if I were you—you don't mind taking a bit of advice, do you?—if I were you, I should get him sorted out right away—*before*. Know what I mean?

Helen (*bemused*) Thank you. I'll remember. Where shall I find him?

Ferris Oh—through there, miss. Up the stairs to the right. Blue door. You can't miss it.

Helen Thank you.

She starts to go, and almost collides with the wall. She lifts her sun-glasses a little to get her bearings, and then goes out up the L stairs. Ferris watches her legs disappearing

Ferris You wouldn't catch *me* sharing a blue room with a man who wouldn't buy me champagne. . . .

He goes out to the kitchen

Lights up in Blue Room. A gentle knock at the door. Geoff gets up, does a few quick exercises and goes to open it. He looks at Helen in her sun-glasses and fails to recognize her

Geoff Yes? Can I help you?

Helen Geoff! Don't be stupid. It's me!

Geoff What?

She lifts her sun-glasses so he can recognize her. He smiles

Helen!

Helen Well, who *else* were you expecting?

She walks into the room, replacing her sun-glasses. He closes the door and follows her

Geoff I didn't recognize you with glasses on.

Helen Well, we've got to be discreet. That's what you said. I didn't want anyone to notice me.

Geoff With them on, they could hardly miss you! (*Indicating the room*) Well? What do you think of it?

Helen What?

Geoff The room.

Helen (*looking around*) It's very dark.

Geoff You've still got your sunglasses on!

Helen (*lifting her glasses for a moment to get a better look*) Oh . . . it's rather blue, isn't it?

Geoff (*a little put out*) Well—it's the Blue Room, isn't it? I mean, that's what it's called—the Blue Room. Here—let me take those from you. (*He takes*

her suitcase and box of chocolates) Oh, that *is* kind! You didn't have to
bring me a present.
Helen I didn't. They're for me.
Geoff For you?
Helen Yes. One of my vices. I always eat chocolates in bed.
Geoff You never told me that ...
Helen (*generously*) You can have some, too.
Geoff Oh. Thanks.

He puts down her suitcase and places her chocolates on the telephone table

Helen It—it seems quite a nice place, doesn't it?
Geoff Well, you chose it, darling.
Helen (*modestly*) I saw it advertised in the parish magazine.

They giggle

Geoff Really? Good lord ...
Helen They said it was very peaceful and isolated.
Geoff It certainly is! If anybody wanted to find us here, they'd have to buy a
compass. Just think of it—two whole days all on our own!
Helen Yes. ...

They look at each other, uncertainly, and go into an awkward kiss. Afterwards ...

Geoff Aren't you going to take them off?
Helen (*blankly*) Sorry?
Geoff Your sun-glasses.
Helen Oh. Yes. I forgot.

She takes them off. They go into another kiss, gradually gaining confidence

*Ferris comes through the swing doors, carrying his screwdriver. He goes off
up the L stairs*

*Helen and Geoff come out of their kiss. She starts to lead him, tentatively,
towards the bed. He holds back*

Geoff Where are we going?
Helen I thought it would be more comfortable over here. Why?
Geoff You ... you haven't unpacked yet.
Helen Well, that won't take me very long. Don't tell me you're nervous!
Geoff (*embarrassed*) Well ... this is a new experience for me.
Helen What?
Geoff I ... I've never done it before.
Helen Done what?
Geoff Slept with a married woman.
Helen Oh, I expect you'll soon get the hang of it ...

They embrace and fall back onto the bed.

Whereupon, Ferris walks in and sees them. He closes the door with a bang.

Geoff and Helen leap apart, nervously. She hastily puts her glasses back on.
They straighten their clothes and tidy themselves up, deeply embarrassed.
Ferris watches in amused silence

Geoff I didn't hear you knock at the door!

Ferris I'm not surprised, the way you were carrying on. You two don't
waste any time, do you? Talk about still waters. And you haven't had
your dinner yet.

Geoff You've no right to come barging in like that.

Ferris I've got to check your telephone. There have been a lot of com-
plaints.

Geoff There'll be some more in a minute!

Ferris Look, I don't want my sister to come back from Frinton and find all
the phones are out of order, do I? And, let's face it, *you* wouldn't like to
reach for *yours* in the middle of the night and find it didn't work, now
would you?

Geoff I won't be needing the telephone in the middle of the night!

Ferris You never know. You might wake up and feel in need of something.
Hot chocolate. Cheese on toast. Anything.

Geoff Will you please go ... !

Ferris All right. All right. I'm going. (*He examines the telephone*) Oh, dear.
This one's out of order, too.

Geoff I told you it was! And you're not doing it now!

Ferris (*replacing the receiver*) You think yourself lucky. You might have
ended up in an hotel that didn't have room service.

Geoff I wish we had ... !

Ferris (*to Helen*) Got your chocolates safe and sound, miss? (*He laughs*)

Geoff Will you get out!

Ferris All right. I'm on my way. (*He turns at the door and looks across at
Helen*) And don't you forget to take your glasses off before you go to bed.
Otherwise something dreadful might happen.

He goes, laughing raucously, and closes the door behind him

Geoff I can't stand that bloke.

Helen Oh, I think he's rather nice. (*Preening*) He thought I was a film star ...

She picks up her suitcase and goes towards the bathroom

Geoff Where are you going?

Helen To have a bath and change for dinner.

Geoff Dinner?

Helen We are going to *eat*, aren't we?

Geoff Oh. Yes—yes, I suppose so ...

She hesitates in the doorway

Helen Didn't you think I was worth it?

Geoff Worth what?

Helen (*unhappily*) Champagne. ...

She goes out and closes the door

Geoff sits, gloomily, on the end of the bed. He sighs and lies back to wait. Lights out in Blue Room

Ferris comes down the L stairs and goes out through the swing door into the kitchen

Lights up in Green Room. Roger sits up and looks at his watch. He gets off the bed, goes to the bathroom door and knocks on it

Roger Are you still there, darling? You're a long time in the bath.
Sally (*off*) I'm making myself beautiful for *you*!
Roger Well, don't take *too* long, will you?

Sally looks out of the bathroom, wrapped in a bath towel

Sally Why don't you order an aperitif? It'll help us work up an appetite.
Roger (*grinning*) My appetite doesn't need working up!
Sally (*with a tolerant smile*) For dinner, darling.

She disappears again, closing the door and almost catching his nose

Roger Ah. Yes. Right. (*He goes to the telephone and lifts the receiver. He has forgotten that it is out of order. He remembers*) Oh, blast! (*He goes out*)

Lights crossfade from Green Room to Blue Room

Helen comes out of the bathroom

Geoff (*sitting up, abruptly*) That was quick.
Helen There isn't any soap.
Geoff Didn't you bring any?
Helen Hotels usually provide soap. (*She collects her sun-glasses and goes to the door*)
Geoff Where are you going?
Helen To *get* some, of course.
Geoff We can ring for room service.
Helen No we can't. The phone doesn't work.

She puts on her sun-glasses and goes out

Geoff lies back on the bed again. Lights out in Blue Room

Roger comes down the R stairs into the reception area, looking for Ferris. No sign of him. He goes to the desk and hits the bell, impatiently

Helen comes down the L stairs into the reception area, with her glasses on. She goes to the desk and addresses Roger's back, thinking he is the waiter

Helen There's no soap in the bathroom ...

Roger turns and sees her. And she sees him! They freeze, staring at each other, unable to believe their eyes

Roger Good lord ... ! You gave me such a shock. You look just like someone I know.

Helen I *am* someone you know! (*She lifts her glasses so that he can recognize her*)

Roger (*appalled*) Helen! (*He looks around, nervously*) What are *you* doing here? I left you at home!

Helen (*replacing her sun-glasses*) Well, you said you'd be away for two days . . .

Roger I *am* away! I'm *here*!

Helen You said it was a business trip.

Roger It is! You don't think I'd come to a place like this for pleasure, do you?

Helen It's a funny place to come on business.

Roger (*glancing around; nervously*) Well, I'm dealing with a funny client. She's very secretive.

Helen Your client's a woman, then?

Roger Ah. Yes. I think so. I mean—yes, she is! And she's very high-powered. Doesn't want anyone to see her. That's why we came here.

Helen How's it all going?

Roger Not very well . . . ! (*He has a sudden thought*) Anyway, what are *you* doing here?

Helen Er . . . w-what? (*She moves away from him, nervously*)

Roger You didn't say *you* were going away, too. Who's looking after my goldfish?

Helen (*reasonably*) Well, I gave him all the ants eggs.

Roger *All* of them? There was enough there for a month! He'll be floating on the top when we get back.

Helen I—er—I thought I'd have a break.

Roger (*casting another nervous glance over his shoulder*) Whatever made you choose this place?

Helen I saw it advertised in the parish magazine.

Roger Yes. So did I . . . !

Helen It said it was secluded. The ideal place to escape.

Roger (*ruefully*) Yes. I know . . . ! (*Pause*) Helen . . .

Helen Yes?

Roger Why are you wearing sun-glasses?

Ferris comes in from the kitchen

Where the hell have you been? I've been waiting for ages.

Ferris I can't be in two places at once, you know. It's hectic is hotel work. My sister never said it would be hectic. (*He sees Helen and goes to her*) Hullo! Had second thoughts already, have you? I'm not surprised. The least you can expect is champagne.

Roger What are you talking about?

Ferris (*continuing to Helen*) You'd have been much better off with *this* one. (*Indicating Roger*) Champagne in the middle of the night, that's his style!

Roger glares at him

Helen (*looking puzzled*) Champagne in the middle of the night? (*She looks, inquiringly, at Roger*)

Roger Ah—yes—for my client! You know how it is in business. Got to keep your client sweet.

Ferris Your client? Don't tell me they *pay* you to do this? (*He nudges Roger and laughs*)

Roger (*abruptly*) Soap!

Ferris What?

Roger (*fiercely*) This young lady. She wanted soap. There isn't any in her bathroom.

Ferris (*turning to Helen again*) Oh, you didn't have to come traipsing down here yourself, miss. You should have sent your Mr Smith down. Or is he already in the bath waiting for the soap? (*He chuckles and goes to get soap from the desk*)

Roger (*puzzled*) Mr Smith? (*He turns to Helen*) What Mr Smith?

Helen Oh—er—the ... the chambermaid!

Roger A chambermaid called Mr Smith?

Helen Yes. He's ... he's a male chambermaid.

Ferris More of a chamber*man*.

Roger (*looking bewildered*) What's a chamberman doing in your bath?

Helen Oh, he's not *in* it! He's just ... seeing to it.

Roger And he's called Smith?

Helen Yes.

Roger Good heavens ...

Ferris returns from the desk

Ferris Yes—quite a coincidence, eh, sir?

Helen What is?

Ferris Well, this gentleman's called Smith, as well.

He indicates Roger, who does not look at all pleased

Helen What are you talking about? *His* name's not Smith.

Ferris It is when he's with a client! (*He laughs, enjoying the situation*)

Roger (*glowering*) Haven't you got anything better to do?

Helen (*to Ferris*) What do you mean?

Ferris Well, you don't think he'd use his real name in a place like this, do you?

Helen Why not?

Ferris He wouldn't want his *wife* to see his name in the register, now would he?

Roger (*seething*) Why don't you go and see to the boiler?

Helen Why shouldn't his wife see his name in the register? After all, business is business.

Roger looks pleased

Ferris Yes—but *his* business is *nobody's* business!

Roger (*looking displeased*) Ferris!

Ferris (*to Helen*) And yours is the same.

Helen Mine?

Ferris Yes—your Mr Smith. They're all the same.

Roger *Her* Mr Smith?

Helen (*loudly*) Soap!!

Ferris Aah!

In his surprise he throws the soap up in the air and Helen catches it

    Anyway, how do *you* know he's not called Smith?

Helen Because I know him.

Ferris (*reacting*) You—you know him?

Helen Yes.

Ferris You mean you two have met before?

Roger Yes. We have . . . !

Ferris Well, fancy you both choosing this place and running into old friends.

Roger She's not an old friend. She's my wife.

Ferris (*not believing his ears*) Your . . . *wife*?

Roger Yes . . . !

Ferris (*to Helen*) He's not your . . . ?

Helen Yes . . . !

Ferris Oh, my good lord . . . ! (*He explodes with laughter*)

Roger It's not funny!

Ferris Oh, yes, it is! I think it's *very* funny! I think it's the funniest thing I've heard for a long time. If only you knew . . . ! (*Confidentially, to Roger*) And there was me saying ——!

Roger Yes! I know what you were saying!

Ferris (*laughing*) Oh, dear, Oh, dear! I shall have to go and make a cup of tea . . . !

He goes out through the swing door, laughing uproariously. He re-appears at once, sees them, goes off into further paroxysms, and disappears again

Roger and Helen are left alone. Both worried, anxious to get away

Roger He's . . . he's easily amused.

Helen Yes. (*Pause*) Well . . . it's very nice to see you, Roger.

Roger Very nice to see you, too.

Helen It was . . . quite a surprise.

Roger It certainly was!

She starts to edge slowly towards the stairs

Helen Well, I—I think I'd better go and have my bath now. I mean, I've got my soap. So I may as well have my bath. Now I've got my soap. Besides, I've got to see to something in the bedroom . . .

Roger And I'd better go and . . . and have a word with my . . . my client. (*He laughs, nervously, as he also edges towards the stairs*)

Helen Er . . . shall I . . . shall I see you later on?

Roger Ah. Yes. Yes, I suppose so. But I'll have to get my client out of the way first.

Helen All right. And I'll get rid of mine.

Roger What?

Helen I mean I'll have my soap—my bath!—with my soap. I . . . I'll keep an eye out for you, then.

Roger Will you? Oh—yes. All right. And I'll keep an eye out for you.
Helen Will you? Oh—yes. All right.

They both make a move. But in the wrong directions. They turn back and collide. Helen drops her soap. They both bend to pick it up and collide again

Sorry.

She rights herself, collects her soap and then they each go quickly out up opposite stairs. Lights up in Blue Room. Helen comes in, carrying her soap. She is still wearing sun-glasses. Geoff sits up as she comes in

Geoff You were a long time.
Helen Was I? (*She closes the door and locks it*)
Geoff (*going to her*) What are you doing?
Helen Locking the door. We don't want that dreadful man bursting in here again, do we?
Geoff Did you find what you wanted?
Helen (*miserably*) No, I didn't!
Geoff You mean there wasn't any?
Helen (*looking at him blankly*) Any what?
Geoff Soap! You were looking for soap. Did you find any?
Helen I found more than I bargained for ... !
Geoff (*puzzled*) More soap?
Helen More of everything! Oh, my God, I *must* have a chocolate. (*She races to her box of chocolates, knocking an ashtray off the table as she does so*)

He picks up the ashtray and watches her in surprise

Geoff Whatever's the matter?
Helen Nothing! Nothing at all. I'll be all right when I've had a chocolate. (*She puts a chocolate into her mouth*)

Geoff goes to her, concerned

Geoff You're not going to eat chocolates *all* the time, are you?
Helen (*chewing*) What?
Geoff Well ... we've only got two days.
Helen Yes. I know. (*Pause*) Geoff ... ?
Geoff Yes?
Helen I've been thinking—if you've never been to bed with a married woman before ... perhaps you shouldn't start now? (*Now rather embarrassed, she heads for the bathroom*)
Geoff Where are you going?
Helen To have a bath. That's why I went to get the soap. (*She opens the bathroom door*)

Geoff smiles, patiently, thinking that he knows the reason for her strange behaviour

Geoff All right, darling! I'll do it.
Helen Do what?
Geoff Order champagne.

She looks puzzled, having forgotten about the champagne, and goes into the bathroom, closing the door behind her

Geoff grins and goes to the telephone. Lights up in Green Room

Roger comes in and locks the door

Sally comes out of the bathroom. She is wearing something brief and sexy, and is painting her fingernails

Sally What on earth are you doing? (*She settles herself in the armchair*)
Roger Locking the door. We don't want that dreadful man bursting in again, do we?
Sally Did you get what you wanted?
Roger No, I didn't!
Sally Oh, darling. . . .

In the Blue Room, Geoff rattles the rest of the receiver, getting no reply. He remembers that it is out of order

Geoff Oh, blast! (*He hangs up and goes out of the door, closing it behind him*)

Lights out in Blue Room. In Green Room, Sally relaxes in a chair, decoratively, painting her nails

Sally I've had such a lovely bath. . . .
Roger Was there any soap?
Sally (*puzzled*) Yes. Of course.
Roger Oh, good.
Sally Darling, are you all right? You look awfully pale. You haven't seen a ghost, have you?
Roger No. This was flesh and blood!
Sally What was?
Roger Oh—er—the chamberman.
Sally (*amused*) What?
Roger Porter!
Sally Ferris?
Roger (*distracted*) No, not him! I think there's another one about.
Sally I wouldn't have thought it was worth having two porters in a place like this. It's not exactly bursting with guests, is it?
Roger Well, there are too many for *my* liking!

Geoff comes down the L stairs into reception, looking for Ferris

Geoff I say . . . ! Anyone about? Ferris! Are you there?

He goes into the restaurant, looking for Ferris

In Green Room

Sally Well, darling? Where did you put them?
Roger (*blankly*) What?
Sally The drinks you went to get. When I was in the bath.
Roger Ah—yes—that's what I went down there for! I knew there was something.

Sally You *are* in a bad way.

Roger I'll ring for room service.

Sally It isn't working.

Roger No. Of course it isn't. I'll go and find Ferris. (*He goes and opens the door*) And, whatever happens, don't open this door to anyone!

Sally Darling ...

Roger Yes?

Sally Perhaps you'd better tie a knot in it.

Roger What?

Sally Your handkerchief. So you remember the drinks this time. (*She smiles, sweetly, at him*)

Roger stumbles out, closing the door behind him. Lights out in Green Room

Geoff comes back into the reception area, not having found Ferris

Roger comes down the R stairs, looking about, furtively. He sees Geoff and goes to him, thinking he is a member of staff

Roger Ah! There you are, waiter!

Geoff (*turning*) I beg your pardon?

Roger (*abruptly*) A gin-and-tonic and a large scotch.

Geoff Sorry?

Roger Come on! Chop-chop! I'm in a hurry.

Geoff I was here first. And first come, first served.

Roger Oh, sorry. I thought you were a waiter.

Geoff Of course I'm not a waiter! I'm *looking* for a waiter.

Roger You mean you're staying here?

Geoff Yes.

Roger So am I.

Roger
Geoff } (*together*) How do you do. (*They shake hands*)

Ferris comes in. He is carrying a mug of tea and is still chuckling to himself. He sees Roger and Geoff together, which sets him off into further paroxysms of mirth

Ferris Oh, dear, Oh, dear ... ! Fancy you two being down here together!

Roger and Geoff cannot understand what is so funny about their being together

Roger What's so funny about that?

Ferris Oh, nothing, sir—nothing at all! (*He tries to control himself*) I'm just having a mug of sweet tea. They say it's very good for shock. (*He offers it to Roger*) Would *you* like some, sir? Right, then—what can I do for you gents? (*He takes a mouthful of tea*)

Geoff Well, as a matter of fact, we're both here for the same thing.

Ferris spits out his mouthful of tea as he starts to laugh again

Ferris Yes, I know! Oh, dear ... ! (*He manages to control his laughter*) You're not both looking for soap, are you?

Roger Certainly not. We want some drinks.

Ferris Right you are, sir. What'll it be?

Geoff (*going to Ferris, tentatively*) I think *I* was here first.

Ferris Don't worry. There's plenty to go around.

Geoff Well, I *am* in a bit of a hurry.

Ferris No, you're not! She'll still be in the bath.

Roger (*looking at Roger with surprise*) Have you got somebody in your bath?

Geoff The—er—chambermaid!

Roger (*grinning*) Are you sure it's not a chamber*man*?

Geoff Certainly not!

Roger Well, what's the chambermaid doing in your bath?

Geoff Cleaning it!

Roger Bit late for cleaning the bath, isn't it, Ferris?

Ferris We're short-staffed, sir. (*With a big smile*) Ah—you two don't know each other, do you? (*He goes between them, crosses his arms and takes their hands*) Mr Smith—meet Mr Smith. (*He brings their hands together and they shake*)

Roger Roger.

Geoff Geoffrey.

Ferris Francis.

Roger So you're the other one!

Geoff (*puzzled*) What?

Roger (*indicating Ferris*) He *said* there were two of us.

Ferris (*to Geoff, taking out his order pad*) What'll it be, then, Mr Smith? As you're in such a tearing hurry.

Geoff (*self-consciously*) Er . . . champagne, please.

Ferris Aah! Changed your mind about the bubbly, then?

Geoff Well . . . I thought perhaps a little champagne *would* be nice.

Ferris You made a wise decision. (*He turns, without thinking, to Roger*) She likes champagne doesn't she, sir?

Roger (*puzzled*) What?

Ferris realizes what he has said and hastily covers up

Ferris I mean they *all* do, don't they? All the young ladies. They all seem to like it.

Roger You mean *he*'s here with a young lady?

Ferris He certainly is!

Geoff Well, you don't have to *tell* everybody . . .

Ferris Why? Is it a secret?

Geoff Of course it's a secret!

Roger (*smiling*) What's she like?

Ferris Very pretty, sir. I'm sure *you*'d like her. (*To Geoff*) I'll have to get the champagne from the cellar, sir.

Roger Champagne, eh? Is it a special occasion, then?

Ferris It certainly is! (*To Geoff, indicating Roger*) He's the expert, you know.

Geoff Expert?

Ferris Oh, yes. He knows what's what all right. Ordered champagne the moment he walked in.

Roger goes to Geoff with a big smile

Roger You're not here with your *wife*, then?
Ferris (*quietly*) No, not *his* wife ... ! (*He laughs*)
Roger Sorry?
Ferris Nothing, sir.
Geoff (*shyly*) No. She's not my wife.
Roger Well, join the club!
Ferris (*To Roger*) What can I get for you, Mr Smith?
Roger Oh—gin-and-tonic and a large Bells, please.
Ferris One G. and T. and a big ding-dong. . . . (*He goes to the drinks trolley, pulls it round in front of the chair and sits down to prepare the drinks*) I'll bring yours up to your room, Mr Smith.
Geoff Beg your pardon?
Ferris The champagne.
Geoff Oh. Yes. Right. (*To Roger, as he starts to go*) I expect I'll see you during dinner?
Roger (*cheerfully*) Yes. We can compare girl-friends.
Ferris (*quietly*) You'll have a nasty surprise if you do ... !

Geoff goes out up the L stairs

   (*Starting to pour a gin-and-tonic—finishing the gin—and whisky*) You know, I don't think he's cut out for this sort of thing.

Roger I don't think *I* am, either ...
Ferris Oh, yes, sir—you've got style. I could tell the moment you walked in.
Roger But that was before my *wife* walked in!
Ferris Don't worry about that, Mr Smith. You'll sort everything out.
Roger You think so? What about dinner?
Ferris I'll book a nice table. The one by the window.
Roger (*desperately*) Ferris—I can't eat down here! My wife might see me!
Ferris I don't expect she'll mind. . . .
Roger Oh, yes, she will! It's no good. I'll have to leave.
Ferris If you go sneaking off in the middle of the night when you're supposed to be here on business it'll only make your wife suspicious. (*He sees that he has poured far too much whisky into the glass and pours some of it back into the bottle*)
Roger But Sally hardly looks like a business client, does she?
Ferris Well, you'll just have to have dinner in your room, won't you? (*He puts the drinks on a small tray*)
Roger Good idea, Ferris! You'll have to do room service. (*He takes the tray of drinks and heads for the stairs*) I'll go and ask her what she wants.
Ferris I *know* what she wants!
Roger (*looking back*) What?
Ferris G. and T. and a big ding-dong!

Music in as Roger goes out up the R stairs

   Ferris replaces the bottles on the trolley and goes out through the swing door, chuckling

Lights up in Blue Room. Geoff comes in and music fades

Helen (*off*) Who is it? Who's out there?
Geoff (*looking surprised*) It's *me*!

Helen comes out of the bathroom. She is now wearing a short néglige, but still has her sun-glasses on

Who did you *think* it was?
Helen I—I didn't know.
Geoff You're not expecting anyone else, are you?
Helen No, of course not!
Geoff Then you must have known it was me.
Helen I couldn't be *sure*, could I? (*She goes to him, urgently*) Did you see anybody down there?
Geoff I saw that dreadful porter.
Helen Ferris?
Geoff Yes.
Helen Anybody else?
Geoff Another man who's staying here. Why?
Helen (*alarmed*) Another *man*?
Geoff Yes.
Helen What did he look like?

Geoff cannot understand her intense interest in a stranger

Geoff What does it matter what he looked like?
Helen Did you *talk* to him?
Geoff (*puzzled by her vehemence*) Well, yes. We did exchange a few words ...
Helen What about?!
Geoff As a matter of fact, we found we had something in common.
Helen Did you?
Geoff Yes. You see—(*he smiles, self-consciously*)—he's calling himself Smith, as well.
Helen (*innocently*) He isn't, is he?
Geoff Yes. Isn't that a coincidence?
Helen You didn't tell him *why* you were calling yourself Smith, did you?
Geoff No, of course I didn't!
Helen That's all right, then ...
Geoff But Ferris did!
Helen What?! Oh, dear ... ! (*She sits on the end of the bed*)
Geoff What's the matter?
Helen I don't feel very well. ...
Geoff I'm not surprised. You've still got your glasses on.

Lights crossfade from Blue Room to Green Room. Roger comes in with the tray of drinks. Sally is draped, gracefully, in the armchair. She looks up as he comes in

Sally You took your time. I thought you'd be rushing back to me.
Roger There was a queue at the bar.

Sally I didn't think there were enough people here to form a queue! Ah—well, at least you've remembered the drinks this time.

Roger Yes. Here we are. (*He hands the gin to her and keeps the whisky*)

Sally Thank you, darling. Well—here's to us! Together. All alone. Just the two of us.

Roger (*doubtfully*) Yes. . . . (*He glances, anxiously, towards the door*)

Sally You don't sound very enthusiastic.

Roger Oh, I expect I'll perk up in a minute. I'm probably hungry.

Sally Good! So am I.

Roger What?

Sally I'm longing for my dinner!

Ferris comes through the swing doors with an ice bucket covered by a napkin, and two glasses. He goes off up the L stairs

Did you book a table?

Roger Well, I . . . I thought perhaps we'd eat up here.

Sally Oh, no, darling. You know I love restaurants. Having dinner's part of the fun. Soft music. Candlelight. Delicious food and wine. . . . (*She gets up and starts to go towards the bathroom with her drink*)

Roger Where are you going?

Sally To dress for dinner, of course.

Roger Oh, I'd much rather eat up here.

Sally You wait till you see my new dress. You'll want to show me off to the other people in the restaurant.

She smiles, confidently, and goes

Roger (*miserably*) Oh, my God . . . ! (*He drinks his whisky in one, and sits on the end of the bed*)

Lights crossfade from Green Room to Blue Room

A knock at the door. Helen looks up, alarmed

Helen There's someone at the door! (*She races towards the bathroom*)

Geoff Where are you going now?

Helen Into the bathroom.

Geoff You've just come *out* of the bathroom!

Helen Well, I don't want anyone to see me like this, do I?

Geoff It'll only be Ferris.

Helen disappears into the bathroom and closes the door

Geoff shrugs, resignedly, and goes to open the door. Ferris comes in with the ice bucket and glasses

Ferris You took your time. I didn't catch you at it again, did I? (*He puts the ice bucket and glasses down on the table*) There we are, sir—one bottle of champagne! (*He produces a quarter bottle of champagne from inside the ice bucket and holds it out with a flourish for Geoff's approval*)

Geoff Oh . . . thanks. (*He looks at the bottle, uncertainly*) Would you . . . would you open it, please?

Ferris Yes, of course, sir. (*He starts to open the bottle*)

Helen comes out of the bathroom, still wearing her néglige and sun-glasses. Ferris sees her, and smiles

Ah, there you are, miss! Have a good bath?

Helen Yes, thank you.

Ferris Plenty of soap?

Helen Er ... yes. Thank you.

Geoff I thought you didn't want anyone to see you dressed like that?

Helen (*calmly*) It's only Ferris.

Geoff cannot understand her change of heart. He turns to Ferris and smiles, nervously

Geoff I told her it would only be you.

Ferris Well, you can't be too careful, sir. *Anyone* might have wandered in. It's surprising, sometimes, who you run into in a place like this. Isn't it, miss? (*He prepares to pull the cork*)

They all anticipate a loud report and tense themselves but the cork comes out silently. Ferris sniffs at it, looks at it disapprovingly and throws it into the icebucket. He wraps the table napkin around the tiny bottle, elaborately, and starts to pour the first glass

Now—I'm keeping a nice table for you two. The one by the window.

Helen Oh, no! I'd rather eat up here!

Ferris What?

Geoff I thought you liked restaurants. Soft music. Candlelight. It's all part of the fun.

Ferris (*dreamily*) Yes, it does get you going. ...

Geoff I wasn't talking to you!

Ferris Oh—sorry. (*He hands a glass of champagne to Helen, smiling warmly at her*) There we are, miss.

Helen Thank you.

Ferris gives Geoff a stern look and goes back to pour the second glass

Helen (*to Geoff*) I don't *want* to eat downstairs!

Geoff Why not?

Helen Well ... we might meet somebody we know.

Geoff (*bewildered*) In this place? It's miles from anywhere! That's why we came here. We're hardly *likely* to run into someone we know.

Ferris (*quietly*) I wouldn't bank on it ... ! (*He finishes pouring the second glass of champagne—which empties the bottle!—and turns the bottle a little as if squeezing out the last drop. He takes the glass to Geoff and hands it to him, rather abruptly*) Champagne for you, Mr Smith!

Geoff Thanks.

Helen I just thought it would be more romantic up here. Just the two of us. Wouldn't it, Mr Ferris?

Ferris Well, yes, but ——

Geoff Will you keep out of this?

Ferris I was only going to say ——
Geoff (*to Helen*) Have you *seen* the restaurant, darling? It's beautiful. You'd like it.
Helen (*uncertainly*) Well . . . I don't know. What do *you* think, Mr Ferris?
Geoff What does it matter what he thinks?
Ferris (*reassuringly*) It's all right, miss. You don't have to worry.
Geoff (*cross*) Do you mind not interrupting all the time?
Ferris (*retaliating*) Well, I was asked! (*Then to Helen, sweetly*) You'll be perfectly safe in the restaurant.
Geoff Why shouldn't she be safe in the restaurant?
Ferris (*continuing*) In fact, you'll probably be the only people in there.
Helen Really?
Ferris Oh, yes. The man in Green, for instance—*he*'s eating in his room.
Helen (*smiling, relieved*) Is he?
Ferris Oh, yes.
Helen Oh, good.
Geoff What the hell does it matter where the man in Green's eating?
Ferris (*turning to Geoff abruptly*) I'll leave you to enjoy your champagne.

Ferris throws the empty bottle disdainfully into the air, catches it in the ice bucket and goes out

Geoff What was that all about?
Helen (*innocently*) I don't know what you mean. (*She drinks her champagne in one and makes for the bathroom again*)
Geoff *Now* where are you off to?
Helen I'm going to get dressed, of course. You did say you wanted to eat in the restaurant, didn't you?

She sails off into the bathroom

Geoff looks after her, puzzled but pleased. He sits on the end of the bed and sips his champagne. Lights out in Blue Room

Ferris comes down the L stairs, puts the ice bucket down on the desk and goes out up the R stairs. Lights up in Green Room. A knock at the door. Roger reacts. He goes, apprehensively, to the door and whispers at it, urgently

Roger Who is it?
Ferris It's me! Ferris! Who do you think it is?
Roger Oh. . . . (*He relaxes and opens the door*)

Ferris comes in

Ferris Sorry, sir. Did I give you a shock?
Roger Yes, you did. You usually walk straight in.
Ferris Well, for all I knew, you might have been *hors de combat* by now. (*He notices that Sally is absent*) Where's the young lady, then?
Roger In the bathroom.
Ferris Not another one in the bathroom? What a very clean class of clientele. What do you fancy, then?
Roger What?

Ferris For dinner. I've brought the menu. (*He takes a battered menu out of his pocket and blows the dust off it*)

Roger Ah. Yes. Well, there may be a bit of a problem about that.

Sally comes out of the bathroom. She is now wearing a stunning dinner dress

Sally There! What do you think of that? (*She pirouettes to show off the dress*)

Roger What? Oh—yes—very nice, darling.

Sally Do *you* like it, Mr Ferris?

Ferris Oh, yes. Very nice. But aren't you a little overdressed for eating in the boudoir?

Sally Don't be silly. We're eating in the restaurant.

Ferris What? (*He glares, angrily, at Roger*) I thought you were eating up here!

Sally Dressed like this?

Ferris But we decided you'd be eating up here. Didn't we, Mr Smith?

Roger Yes, we did!

Sally I don't care what you two decided. *I've* decided we're eating downstairs.

Roger But, darling, I did rather *hope* we'd eat up here.

Ferris So did I. I've brought the menu. (*He blows some more dust off the menu and thrusts it towards her*)

Sally Well I want to eat in the restaurant. (*She pushes the menu away*)

Ferris Oh, you wouldn't like it down there, miss. It'll be very crowded. (*He thrusts the menu again*)

Sally Crowded? The hotel's almost empty! (*She pushes the menu away again*)

Ferris It may be empty now, but there'll be people arriving later. My sister told me she always gets lots of people arriving on Fridays. They come down from the suburbs, you know. Dozens of them. All frantic for food.

Roger And we don't want a lot of hungry trippers spoiling our evening, do we, darling?

Ferris No, of course we don't! (*He forces the menu on to Sally*)

Roger It'll be much nicer up here in our room. It'll be—romantic!

Sally Oh, Roger, we've plenty of time for that! (*She gives him the menu*) I'm all dressed up now—and *I'm* going to eat in the restaurant!

She sweeps out, closing the door behind her. Roger hands the menu back to Ferris, abruptly, and clings on to him, desperately

Roger Ferris! My wife's down there!

Ferris I know!

Roger You'll have to do something.

Ferris *Me*?

Roger Yes!

Ferris Why me?

Roger That's what hotel management's all about. Looking after the customers. Didn't your sister tell you that?

Ferris No . . .

During this Sally comes down the R stairs into the reception area. She goes and peers, hopefully, at the drinks trolley

Roger Well, it's true! And I'm a customer, so look after me!
Ferris Oh, no-no—I couldn't do that . . .

Roger takes a five-pound note out of his pocket and holds it out to Ferris, who looks at it, suspiciously

You wouldn't be trying to bribe me, would you, sir?
Roger Yes!
Ferris I'll see what I can do. (*He takes the five-pound note, abruptly, and goes out, closing the door behind him*)
Roger Oh, my God . . . ! (*He sits on the bed, despondently*)

Ferris comes racing down the R stairs into the reception area. He sees Sally, laughs nervously, and is about to go when she speaks

Sally Ferris!
Ferris Yes, miss?
Sally I should like a gin-and-tonic.
Ferris (*abruptly*) You've just had one! (*He continues on his way*)
Sally Ferris!

Ferris stops impatiently

I want another.
Ferris I'm in a hurry!
Sally So am I!
Ferris Well, help yourself!
Sally The bottle's empty.
Ferris Oh, all right! I won't be a minute.

He goes, distractedly, out through the swing door

Sally looks surprised by his behaviour. She goes across to sit on the low sofa

Lights up in Blue Room. Helen comes out of the bathroom. She has changed into a pretty dress. Geoff looks at her and smiles, appreciatively

Geoff I say, that's nice! You *are* dressed up, aren't you? You'll put me to shame. I'd better go and put my jacket on.
Helen I'll wait for you downstairs. (*Meaning: to make sure the coast is clear*)
Geoff (*surprised*) I shan't be a second.
Helen I'd rather wait downstairs, darling.
Geoff Well, I tell you what—order some more champagne, eh? (*He grins happily*)
Helen Right!

He struts off into the bathroom

Helen goes to open the door to the corridor, has slight misgivings and puts her sun-glasses on before going out and closing the door behind her

In Green Room. Roger gets off the bed, miserably

Roger Oooooh ... ! I think I'm going to be ill. ...

He goes out into the bathroom

Helen comes racing down the L stairs. She trips, reaches out to save herself but misses the desk and grabs the ice bucket instead. She staggers towards Sally, clutching the ice bucket. Sally looks surprised

Sally Good-evening!
Helen Oh ... good-evening.

Sally thinks it rather strange for Helen to be wearing sun-glasses

Sally Do you find the lights a little bright?
Helen Oh ... no. Is the restaurant through there? (*Without waiting for a reply, she thrusts the ice bucket into Sally's hands*)

Helen runs out into the restaurant

Ferris comes swiftly in through the swing door with a new bottle of gin. He goes to where he left Sally, finds she has gone, looks about and sees her. He trots across to her

Ferris (*abruptly*) There! Gin! (*He thumps the gin down beside her, grabs the ice bucket from her and goes racing out up the L stairs*)

Sally looks astonished

Helen comes back from the restaurant

Helen (*relieved*) There's nobody in there.
Sally I'm not surprised ... !

Helen sits down near the drinks trolley, away from Sally

In the Blue Room, the door bursts open and Ferris staggers in, breathlessly

Geoff comes out of the bathroom, putting on his jacket

Geoff Ferris! Whatever's the matter?
Ferris Bad news, sir!
Geoff Bad news?
Ferris The restaurant!
Geoff What about it?
Ferris It's shut.
Geoff It's only just opened.
Ferris Well, now it's shut again! You'll have to eat up here.
Geoff What?
Ferris Well, you can't eat down there if it's shut, can you? (*He looks about*) Has the young lady gone back into the bathroom again?
Geoff No. She's gone downstairs.
Ferris Downstairs?!
Geoff Yes. I told her to order more champagne.
Ferris (*in despair*) Oh, no ... !
Geoff I thought you'd be pleased.

Ferris (*firmly*) *You—wait—here!*
Geoff What?

Ferris races out again

    Geoff watches him go in astonishment. He shrugs, starts to take off his jacket and goes out into the bathroom

In the reception area . . .

Sally Have you ever been here before?
Helen No. It's my first time.
Sally Same here . . .

Ferris comes racing down the L *stairs. He sees Helen*

Ferris Ah! there you are! (*To Sally*) Excuse me. (*He goes and grabs Helen's hand and starts to drag her out*)
Helen (*protesting*) What *are* you doing?
Sally Whatever's going on?

Sally watches in surprise as Ferris drags Helen out up the L *stairs, Sally reaches for the bottle of gin*

    In Green Room. Roger comes out of the bathroom carrying a glass of fizzing Alka-Seltzer. He sits on the end of the bed again, contemplating the drink, mournfully

In Blue Room. The door bursts open and Ferris comes in, dragging the astonished Helen behind him. He closes the door and leans against it, breathing heavily, trying to get his breath

Helen Have you gone mad? What's all this about?
Ferris (*hushed and urgent*) You can't eat down there!
Helen You said I'd be safe in the restaurant.
Ferris Well, you're not! *He's* going to be there.
Helen Who?
Ferris Your husband!
Helen You said he was eating in his room.
Ferris Well, he's changed his mind! Now he's going to eat in the restaurant!
Helen Oh, no!
Ferris Oh, yes! So you'll have to eat up here. (*He fans his face with the menu*)

    Geoff comes out of the bathroom

Ferris tries to look relaxed, though he is still gasping

Geoff Ah! You found her all right, then?
Ferris Oh, yes. She hadn't gone far.
Geoff (*to Helen*) Did he tell you about the restaurant?
Helen Yes, he certainly did!
Geoff Isn't it dreadful?
Helen It could have been worse . . . !
Ferris You'll be much safer up here.

Geoff Safer?

Ferris Better! (*Hustling them both to the bed and pushing them, unceremoniously, on to it*) Much better up here. In your own little nest. Just the two of you. All on your own. I'll be back in a minute! (*He goes staggering out, breathlessly, closing the door behind him*)

Geoff I can't think what he's in such a state about.

Helen *I* can ...!

Geoff Oh, well—never mind, eh? It can't be helped. After all, we came here to be together, and now we're going to *be* together.

Tentatively, he tries to embrace her, but she escapes from underneath him and he falls face down on the bed

Helen I'd better have another chocolate! (*She heads for the chocolates*)

Geoff follows her, bewildered

Geoff Darling ——

Helen Yes?

Geoff Is something wrong?

Helen No—no, of course not ... (*Then she turns to face him in sudden desperation*) Yes, there is!

Geoff But I thought you were looking forward to tonight.

Helen I was! I was! (*Tearfully*) But it's no good. I don't think I can go through with it ...!

Helen runs out into the bathroom

Geoff What?!

Ferris races down the L stairs, stops, sees Sally, giggles, and races off up the R stairs. She looks after him, bemused by his antics, and pours more gin

In Blue Room, Helen races out of the bathroom with her case and clothes and starts hastily packing.

Geoff stares at her, bewildered and frustrated

Geoff Whatever's the matter? What's got into you?

Helen I just can't stand the subterfuge ...!

Geoff Don't be silly, darling! We're not married to each other, so there's *bound* to be subterfuge. But it's nothing to worry about!

Helen But I've never done this sort of thing before!

Geoff (*wildly*) Neither have I! But there's got to be a first time for everything! It'll be all right—you see. We'll have some food and a lot of wine, and it'll all be wonderful! (*Singing*) "Wunderbar, wunderbar ..."

Helen No, it won't! It won't!

She makes for the door, her suitcase bursting with clothes. He is appalled

Geoff Where the hell are you off to now?

Helen I'm going h—o—o—o—m—e! (*She goes out of the door*)

Geoff Oh, Helen!

She closes the door in his face

Oh, *hell!*

He goes out into the bathroom. Lights out in Blue Room

Helen runs down the L stairs, sees Sally, feels embarrassed, tries to pull herself together, and runs off up the R stairs. Sally looks even more surprised, pours herself a large gin and goes to the trolley for tonic

In Green Room, the door opens and Ferris comes in, breathlessly. Roger gets up from the end of the bed with his Alka-Seltzer

Ferris (*cheerfully*) It's all right, Mr Smith. You can relax now.
Roger Are you sure?
Ferris Of course I'm sure. She's going to have dinner in her room.
Roger (*cheering up*) Oh, good! Well done, Ferris! (*He takes another five pound note out and gives it to Ferris*)
Ferris Oh, thank you, sir!

The door opens and Helen comes in, carrying her suitcase and still wearing her sun-glasses. Ferris and Roger look at her in surprise

Roger Helen! What are you doing in *here*?
Helen Well, I thought I may as well move in with *you*. (*She plonks her case down on the bed*)

Ferris and Roger look at each other, appalled. Roger grabs back the five pound note. Ferris takes the Alka-Seltzer from Roger and starts to drink it

Black-out

CURTAIN

ACT II

The same. A few moments later.

Ferris is holding the empty glass, still breathless from running up and down the stairs. Roger is frozen with fear. Helen is unpacking her clothes on the bed, unaware of any atmosphere. Sally is sitting with her gin. Helen looks at Roger

Helen Darling . . . ?
Roger Yes?
Helen You're awfully quiet.
Ferris He's trying to remember the Lord's Prayer.

Helen goes to Roger

Helen You are glad to see me, aren't you?
Roger Of course I am, darling!
Ferris *Are* you?
Roger (*to Ferris, fiercely*) Of course I am! (*Then to Helen*) In a way.
Helen In a way?
Roger Well . . . it is a little . . . inconvenient.
Ferris It certainly is . . . !
Helen Why? Husband and wife usually share the same room, don't they?
Roger Yes. Yes, I know that, darling. But, you see, I do have to think about my client.
Ferris You certainly do! She's downstairs, waiting for you!
Helen (*calmly*) That's all right. You go ahead.
Roger What?
Helen You go and talk business with your client. I'll wait for you up here. (*She goes back to her clothes on the bed*)

Roger exchanges a look with Ferris

Roger Ah. Well . . .
Helen Isn't that a good idea?
Roger No. Not very.
Helen Why not? Mr Ferris can bring me a sandwich and I'll curl up here until you've finished.
Ferris If you're curled up here, he won't be *able* to finish . . .

Roger goes to Helen urgently

Roger I tell you what! You go back to your room—just for tonight—and we'll meet each other tomorrow. How about that? (*He smiles, hopefully*)

Helen throws herself face-down on the bed, kicks her legs and wails in apparent despair

Helen You're turning me out!

Roger What?

Helen Your own wife! You're turning me out of the nuptial bed!

Roger Well, I wasn't thinking of it as the nuptial bed exactly.

Ferris Neither was I!

Roger And of course I'm not turning you out.

Ferris Aren't you?

Roger (*to Ferris, fiercely*) No, of course not! Not turning her out like *that*. I'm just ... asking her to go. For the time being.

Ferris Oh, I see. Not turning her out. Just getting her out.

Roger Precisely!

Ferris (*quietly*) Well, I should get her out quick before your "client" comes looking for you.

Roger Oh, my God ... ! Look, Ferris—you go down and make sure she's got a drink. And nuts and things. (*He urges Ferris towards the door*)

Ferris Nuts and things?

Roger (*impatiently*) You know what nuts are!

Ferris Yes, but I don't think that's what she's looking for at the moment.

Roger Of course she is! Everyone likes nuts. Tell her I'll be there in a minute. Keep her entertained.

Ferris (*doubtfully*) Well, I'll do my best, sir. But I'm not very good with nuts.

Ferris goes, closing the door behind him

Roger goes back to Helen. She looks up at him, all sweet innocence

Helen I haven't put you out, have I, darling?

He reacts and sits beside her. Lights out in Green Room

Ferris comes down the R *stairs into the reception area. Sally looks up as he approaches*

Ferris Sorry about that, miss.

Sally What on earth were you doing, dragging that poor girl out of here like that?

Ferris She'd lost her way. Didn't know which room she was supposed to be in.

Sally And have you got it sorted out now?

Ferris I'm not sure ... ! (*He glances, anxiously, towards the stairs*)

Sally (*patiently*) Well, now you're here do you think you could stop long enough to pour me a drink?

Ferris Yes, of course, miss ...

Sally A large gin-and-tonic.

Ferris Another one? Good Lord ... (*He pours, liberally, from both bottles at once*)

Sally I can't think what Roger's doing up there all this time.

Ferris Oh, he ... he's just sorting one or two things out.

Sally What's he got to sort out?

Ferris Here we are, miss—large G. and T.

Ferris goes toward the restaurant, holding the drink above his head. Sally looks cross

Sally Ferris! I'm over here.

Ferris I thought you'd prefer to have it in the restaurant.

Sally Why?

Ferris It's much nicer in there. Soft music, candlelight . . .

Sally (*fed up*) Oh, all right! It can't be worse than sitting here all on my own.

Sally goes out to the restaurant

Ferris casts another anxious look towards the stairs and starts to follow her

Ferris Perhaps you'd like a few nuts, miss?

Ferris goes out after Sally

Lights up in Green Room. Helen is still lying on the bed. Roger is sitting beside her

Roger You see darling—I could be on to a very good thing tonight.

Helen What?

Roger A very big deal! If only we can get together on it . . .

Helen Why shouldn't you get together on it? You're a good businessman. You usually get what you want.

Roger Ah. Yes. But if my . . . client found out that my wife was here, it might not be too *good* for business.

Helen Why not?

Roger Well . . . (*he bends over her and fondles her shoulders with husbandly affection*) . . . you see—she's one of those ladies who do like to mix business with . . . with the other thing. (*He kisses the top of her head*)

Helen (*wide eyed*) Really?

Roger Oh, yes. And the problem is—(*he smiles, modestly*)—and you're going to find this very difficult to believe—she does rather fancy me.

Helen *You?*

Roger There! I knew you'd be surprised!

Helen (*sitting up and looking at him*) But what does it matter if she fancies you?

Roger (*with difficulty*) Ah—well, you see—sometimes in business you have to . . . string people along a bit.

Helen Well, string her along, then! I'll wait here until you've got rid of her.

Roger But that's the problem. In order to—to finalize the deal, she might *insist* on . . . on coming up here.

Helen (*astonished*) To your bedroom?

Roger For a nightcap. Before going to bed.

Helen What?!

Roger (*hastily*) Before she goes to her room—to bed! And it would . . . hamper things a little if she came up here—for a nightcap—and found my wife sitting here.

Helen Oh, I see ... Yes, I suppose that *would* be embarrassing. (*She smiles, reassuringly, and puts her arms around him*) Well, you don't have to worry, darling.
Roger (*relieved*) Oh, good!
Helen I'll wait in the bathroom till you've finished.

Roger reacts. Lights out in Green Room

Ferris comes out of the restaurant, muttering to himself

Ferris I never can find my nuts when I want them ...

Geoff comes racing down the L stairs, looking for Helen. He sees Ferris and runs to him

Geoff Have you seen her?
Ferris Who?
Geoff Helen!
Ferris (*innocently*) Isn't she with you?
Geoff If she was with me I wouldn't be looking for her, would I? She just got up, grabbed her clothes and ran out!
Ferris And didn't she say where she was going?
Geoff She *said* she was going home, but she can't have been because I can still see her car outside. So she must be here somewhere. (*He runs towards the restaurant*)
Ferris (*quietly*) Yes, she is ... !

Geoff stops and runs back to Ferris

Geoff Yes, she is?
Ferris Well she must be if her car's still outside. Don't worry. She's bound to turn up sooner or later.
Geoff I'll just have to go on looking. (*He starts to go again, but stops, abruptly, as he has a sudden thought*) Ah!
Ferris (*jumping*) Aah!

Geoff runs back to Ferris

Geoff There's something she *might* come back for.
Ferris Is there? What?
Geoff (*delightedly*) She left her chocolates behind!

He runs out up the L stairs, optimistically

Sally comes in from the restaurant

Sally Ferris!
Ferris Nuts?
Sally Yes. Nuts—now!

Sally goes back into the restaurant

Ferris Nuts now. Right.

Ferris collects a bowl of nuts from the drinks trolley and follows Sally back into the restaurant

Lights up in Green Room. Roger gets up from the bed

Roger Oh, come on, darling! It won't be for long. I'll give you a hand with these. (*He starts to repack her clothes*)

Helen No! I can't go back to my room!

Roger Why not?

Helen (*improvising*) There—there was a man there!

Roger A man?

Helen He just burst in. Kicked the door open and burst in! (*Overdoing it a little*) I was so frightened . . . !

Roger What did he want?

Helen He said he was looking for the bathroom.

Roger Well, that wasn't very frightening. The poor fellow was probably lost. Anxious for ablutions.

Helen (*hurt*) Roger! He wasn't *really* looking for a bathroom.

Roger What *was* he looking for?

Helen What do you think!

Roger (*appalled*) Good Lord! He wasn't after that, was he?

Helen Yes!

Roger I've told you before. You *must* leave your Post Office Savings book at home.

Helen stands on the bed and jumps up and down, furiously

Helen He was after *me*!

Roger Well, how did you get rid of him?

Helen I said that if he didn't go away at once, I'd call my husband.

Roger (*alarmed*) But that's *me*!

Helen Exactly!

Roger And did he go?

Helen Yes . . .

Roger (*pleased*) Oh. Good!

Helen But he might come back again! (*Putting her arms around him*) That's why I decided to move in with you. I thought I'd be safer here than all alone in *my* room.

A knock at the door. Helen jumps up into Roger's arms

That'll be him! He's followed me! Darling, you'll have to get rid of him.

Roger Will I?

Helen Well, I am your wife, and husbands are supposed to protect their wives.

Roger Are they? I don't remember that in the marriage service. Love, honour and obey was enough to be going on with. (*He puts her down*)

Helen heads for the bathroom

Where are you going?

Helen To hide in the bathroom.

Roger (*alarmed*) No! You mustn't go in there!

Helen Why not?

Roger It's rather untidy.

Helen That doesn't matter. Get rid of him!

She closes the bathroom door behind her

Roger (*distraught*) Oh, my God . . . !

Another knock at the door

All right! I'm coming!

Roger hastily gathers up Helen's clothes, kneels down and pushes them under the bed. Then he opens the door, still on his knees

Geoff is there. He looks surprised to find Roger in such a position

What the hell do *you* want?
Geoff (*nervously*) Can I come in for a minute?
Roger Why not? Everybody else has!

Geoff closes the door, and as Roger has remained on his knees, Geoff kneels down also, facing Roger

Geoff I'm looking for my girl-friend.
Roger Well, you won't find her in here. (*He gets up*)
Geoff I've lost her.
Roger Lost her?
Geoff (*scrambling to his feet*) Yes. I've been searching all over. You haven't seen her, have you?
Roger How do *I* know? I don't know what your girl-friend looks like, do I?
Geoff Ah—no—of course not. I'd forgotten.
Roger Look, I would ask you to stay for a drink, but I am in a bit of a hurry. . . .
Geoff Yes—of course you are. I'm so sorry. I didn't mean to delay you. (*He is about to go, but looks about*) Is everything all right with yours? *Yours* hasn't disappeared, as well, has she?
Roger Ssh!

He grabs Geoff and puts one hand quickly over his mouth to silence him. Geoff's eyes are wide with astonishment. Roger casts a nervous glance towards the bathroom, then looks at Geoff again

What are you talking about?

Geoff pulls Roger's hand away from his mouth so he can speak

Geoff *Yours*! You know! Your girlfr ——!

Roger hastily puts his hand back over Geoff's mouth

Roger You mean my *wife*! I'm here with my *wife*!

Geoff, still gagged, shakes his head, vigorously. Roger nods his head, equally vigorously. Geoff's eyes show his bewilderment. Roger hisses at him

She's *here*!

Geoff looks appalled. Roger removes his hand from Geoff's mouth and puts one finger to his own lips, asking for silence

Geoff (*in a whisper*) Your ... wife?!

Roger nods and jerks his head towards the bathroom

Roger In there.
Geoff In the bathroom?
Roger Yes.
Geoff Good lord ... ! Did you *know* she was coming?
Roger Of course I didn't, you bloody fool!

> *Ferris comes out of the restaurant in a hurry. He is heading for the stairs as Sally comes out after him*

Sally Ferris!

Ferris stops apprehensively

Ferris Yes, miss?
Sally Where are you going now?
Ferris (*fed up*) Well, you've had your nuts! What more do you want?
Sally More gin.
Ferris Yes, I thought you would ... ! I'll be back in a minute.
Sally (*severely*) Well, don't keep me waiting for long.

> *She goes back into the restaurant*

Ferris races out up the R stairs

In Green Room

Geoff (*whispering, urgently*) But if your wife's in *here*, what are you going to do about the one downstairs?
Roger Exactly! That's the problem! (*Then he has a sudden idea*) Here—wait a minute. . . . (*He looks at Geoff, a smile of hope beginning to show*) I say, this *is* a bit of luck. . . .
Geoff What is?
Roger You being left in the lurch. It could be a blessing in disguise.
Geoff (*puzzled*) Could it? Who for?
Roger Well, for me, of course! (*He casts a quick glance towards the bathroom*) You can pretend that *my* girl-friend is *your* girl-friend.

Geoff sits on the chair, considering this

Geoff But ... what about *my* girl-friend?
Roger You said you'd lost her.
Geoff Yes. But I hope she'll turn up again. *Then* what happens?
Roger Let's worry about one thing at a time, shall we?

The door opens and Ferris comes in, breathlessly, talking as he enters

Ferris Mr Smith! You'd better hurry up or ... ! (*He stops as he sees Geoff and reacts*) Mr Smith! What are *you* doing in here?

Roger He's looking for his girl-friend.
Ferris (*alarmed*) She's not in here, is she?
Roger Of course she's not in here.
Ferris Thank God for that!
Roger He doesn't know *where* she is.
Ferris (*pointedly*) No, but *you* know where *yours* is, don't you?
Roger Yes—downstairs!
Ferris Well she's had a lot of gin and she's getting very persistent. If you
  don't go down there soon, *she*'ll be coming up *here*!

Geoff has been deep in thought and now looks up with sudden inspiration

Geoff I say—Ive got an idea!
Roger Oh. Good.
Geoff Why don't I stay here and talk to your wife while you go downstairs
  and see to your girl-friend then if *my* girl-friend turns up again while
  you're downstairs talking to *your* girl-friend then at least *I'll* only be
  talking to somebody else's wife.

*Ferris and Roger have been watching Geoff, amazed at his exposition. They
exchange a surprised look*

Ferris I think I've lost track of the conversation. (*Indicating Roger*) His wife
  isn't here.
Geoff Yes, she is!
Ferris (*turning to Roger*) Is she?
Roger (*patiently*) Ferris, you know very well she is.
Ferris Yes. *I* know that, and *you* know that, but I didn't think *he* knew that!
Geoff He just told me.
Ferris Did you?
Roger Yes.
Ferris I think I'm getting one of my headaches. . . .
Roger Good heavens! I'd better let my wife out of the bathroom. (*He starts
  to go*)
Ferris (*alarmed*) What?!

*Ferris rushes across and intercepts the astonished Roger. As Roger tries to get
past him, they take a few steps up and down in unison, almost as if they were
dancing. They pause for a moment*

  Just once more then I really must go.

They execute a few more steps, then Roger pulls away and glares at him

Roger What's the matter with you?
Ferris Are you trying to tell me that your wife is in the bathroom?
Roger Yes.
Ferris *This* bathroom?
Roger Yes!
Ferris And you're going to let her *out* of the bathroom?
Roger Of course! She was only hiding from *him*.
Ferris I'm not surprised!

Geoff What?

Roger She thought he was a sex maniac.

Ferris And she's hiding in there?

Roger Yes. But now she can come out because there's no danger.

Ferris There will be if she does!

Roger Don't be silly, Ferris. I want to introduce her to Mr Smith. There's nothing dangerous about that.

Ferris Oh, yes, there is . . . !

Roger Get out of the way, Ferris! (*He pushes Ferris out of the way*)

Ferris ends up on Geoff's knee, reacts and hastily moves away. Roger opens the bathroom door

It's all right, darling! You can come out now.

Helen comes out of the bathroom backwards, her sun-glasses now on the back of her head

Geoff stares at her, unable to believe his eyes, and rises, as if in a trance

Geoff Did you say that . . . that this is your *wife*?

Roger Yes. Of course.

Geoff I don't think I feel very well . . . (*He goes to the bed and sinks on to it in despair*)

Ferris Neither do I . . . ! (*He goes and sits with Geoff*)

Helen (*turning and seeing Geoff*) Aaaaaah! (*She hastily puts her sun-glasses on correctly and rushes away, fearfully*)

Roger (*following her*) Darling, whatever's the matter?

Helen It's him!

Roger Who?

Helen The one who burst into my bedroom! (*She affects a tear and sinks into the armchair*) Aaaaaaah . . . !

Roger kneels beside her to comfort her

Roger It's all right darling. There's nothing to be frightened of . . . (*He pats her on the knee*)

Geoff utters a little moan

Ferris (*comforting him*) It's all right, darling. There's nothing to be frightened of . . . (*He pats him on the knee*)

Helen Aaaaah! (*She cries even louder*)

Roger Darling, there's nothing to worry about. There, there . . . ! (*He puts his arm around her and rocks her, comfortingly*)

Geoff utters another small moan

Ferris Darling, there's nothing to worry about. There, there . . . ! (*He puts his arm around Geoff and rocks him, comfortingly*)

Helen Aaaah!

Roger You mustn't get so upset. . . . (*He kisses her briefly on the lips*)

Ferris considers this in silence for a moment, then makes a supreme effort . . .

Ferris You mustn't get so upset ... (*He starts to turn towards Geoff, but hastily thinks better of it*)

Roger He's not really a sex maniac. The poor chap was only looking for his girl-friend.

Helen R-really?

Roger Yes. She walked out on him. That's right isn't it, Geoff?

Geoff It certainly is! She just got up and walked out. (*He gives Helen a beady look*) Can *you* imagine anyone doing a thing like that?

Ferris And after he'd bought her champagne, as well.

Helen I expect she had a very good reason. (*But she has the good grace to look a little shame-faced*)

Roger Perhaps she was frightened that her husband might find out! (*He laughs*)

Geoff Aah! I think I'd better be going. (*He makes for the door, anxious to escape*)

Roger Aren't you going to stay here and talk to my wife?

Geoff No! I've changed my mind! (*He stumbles out, closing the door behind him*)

Roger Poor little chap. He's in a bit of a state.

Ferris (*quietly*) I'm not surprised. ... !

Geoff staggers down the R stairs, gathers his breath and runs out up the L stairs. He comes into the Blue Room, hesitates and goes out into the bathroom

Roger (*standing up, hopefully*) Well, that's all right, then, isn't it, darling? He wasn't a sex maniac, after all. So now you can safely go back to *your* room.

Helen No, I can't I'm staying here with you.

Roger exchanges a look of panic with Ferris

Ferris I'd better go and give your client some more nuts. ... (*He heads for the door*)

Helen By the way, darling ...

Roger Yes?

Helen (*puzzled*) Did you know that there are some ladies clothes in your bathroom?

Ferris slams the door and returns, anxiously

Roger (*innocently*) In ... in *this* bathroom?

Helen Yes.

Roger Ladies clothes? Are you sure?

Helen Well, go and look.

Roger Ferris—go and look.

Ferris (*aside to Roger*) I don't need to look. They're ladies clothes all right!

Roger (*aside to Ferris*) They're Sally's clothes!

Ferris (*aside to Roger*) Yes, I know. ... !

Helen Well? Who do they belong to?

Roger Ah. Well. Now let me see. . . . (*He has an idea, and a big smile spreads across his face as he turns to look at Ferris*) Of course! They belong to Ferris.

Ferris reacts and glares at Roger. Helen rises, astonished

Ferris Pardon?

Roger smiles back, innocently. Helen looks at Ferris in total astonishment

Helen To *you*?
Ferris (*vehemently*) No, they don't!
Roger Yes, they do! (*Unseen by Helen, he takes out some money and puts it into Ferris's hand*)
Ferris (*looking at the money unimpressed*) No, they don't!

Roger hastily takes out some more money and thrusts it into Ferris's hand

Roger Yes, they do!

Ferris looks at it, better pleased, and turns to Helen, sombrely

Ferris Yes, they do . . .
Helen Those clothes out there belong to *you*?
Ferris Yes, miss. I'm afraid so . . .
Helen (*incredulously*) You don't . . . *wear* them, do you?
Ferris (*outraged*) No! Of course I don't!
Roger Yes, you do! (*Unseen by Helen, he again pushes some money into Ferris's hand*)

Ferris looks at it, again unimpressed

Ferris No, I don't!

Roger, furious with Ferris, hastily pushes some more money into his hand

Roger Yes, you do!

Ferris looks at it, better pleased, and turns to Helen

Ferris Yes, I do.
Helen Often?
Roger (*firmly*) Every Saturday night.
Ferris (*glaring at Roger*) What!
Roger He likes to entertain the guests during dinner. You do a sort of cabaret act, don't you, Ferris?
Ferris No, I do *not*!

Desperately, Roger pushes a handful of notes into Ferris's hand. Reluctantly, Ferris attempts a song

"What good is sitting alone in your room? Come join the cabaret. . . ."

Sally comes out of the restaurant, carrying an empty glass, looking for Ferris

Sally Ferris!

No sign of him. She goes to the trolley, tops up her gin, drinks it in one and puts down the glass. Then she goes out, purposefully, up the R stairs

Ferris abandons his song and sits on the bed wearily

Helen But, Mr Ferris—how did your clothes get into Roger's bathroom?
Ferris *I* don't know! You'd better ask him!

He looks at Roger, passing the buck. Roger improvises, desperately

Roger Ah—well—they were decorating.
Ferris Who were?
Roger Small men in white coats! (*To Helen*) Men with brushes.
Helen Painting?
Roger Yes. *His* room. So I said he could keep his dresses here. Well, you wouldn't like *your* dresses smelling of paint, would you? (*He turns to Ferris, urgently*) But you can't leave them here!
Ferris Oh, yes, I can! (*He starts to go*)
Roger (*following him*) But my *wife's* here now, isn't she? And we don't want your clothes mixed up with hers, do we? So you'd better remove them!
Ferris (*belligerently*) Well, where am I going to put them?
Roger You'll think of something!
Ferris No, I won't!
Roger Yes, you will!
Ferris No, I won't!

Furiously Roger takes out some money and thrusts it at Ferris

Roger Yes, you . . . ! (*He assumes that it is too little and produces some more money*)
Ferris (*taking it*) Yes, I will . . .

Ferris goes into the bathroom

As the door closes, the other door opens and Sally comes storming in, fed up with being kept waiting

Sally How much longer are you going to keep me waiting?
Roger Ah—yes—I'm awfully sorry. I—I had something to see to.
Sally (*glaring at Helen*) And what are *you* doing in here? You may not know which room you're supposed to be in, but it certainly isn't *this* one!
Helen Sorry?
Roger (*intervening, hastily*) She's not staying!
Sally She'd better not be.
Roger She just popped in to—to ask the way.
Sally Yes, I bet she did!
Helen Are you the one who was waiting for him downstairs?
Sally Yes, I am!
Helen (*with a big smile*) Ah! So you must be his client? (*She goes and sits on the bed*)
Sally Is *that* what he told you?

Roger intervenes again

Roger (*to Sally*) Look—I shan't be very long. Wouldn't you like to go downstairs again?

Sally No, I would not! What's *she* doing here?

Roger Ah—well—you see . . . (*He tries to ingratiate himself*) I hope you got yourself a drink while you were waiting.

Sally Yes, I did. Two or three, as a matter of fact.

Roger Oh, good.

Sally Well, Roger—I'm waiting.

Roger Ah—for dinner, yes.

Sally No—for introductions and explanations. Who is she and what the hell is she doing in this room?

But before Roger has to reply, Ferris walks out of the bathroom with an armful of clothes

Sally (*looking at him in surprise*) Ferris! What *are* you doing?

Ferris sees her, and goes to her, urgently

Ferris I left you downstairs. You haven't run out of nuts, have you?

Sally No, but I *have* run out of patience.

Ferris I thought you would. (*To Roger*) I said she would.

Sally Where are you going with those clothes?

Ferris I . . . I'm moving them, miss.

Sally *I* didn't ask you to move them.

Helen Why should you?

Sally Because they happen to be mine!

Roger and Ferris exchange a frantic look

Helen (*puzzled*) Yours?

Sally Yes.

Helen No, they're not. They belong to Mr Ferris.

Sally tries to comprehend what she is hearing

Sally To . . . to *him*? (*She looks at Ferris*)

Ferris (*nodding, embarrassed*) Yes. That's why I was moving them.

Roger and Ferris are trying desperately to think of a way out

Sally But they're *women*'s clothes, Ferris.

Ferris Yes, madam . . .

Sally (*as if to a child*) You don't wear women's clothes, Ferris.

Ferris Apparently I do on a Saturday, miss.

Sally (*erupting*) Don't be ridiculous! (*She looks at Roger*) Look, I don't know what this is all about, but you know as well as I do that those clothes belong to me!

Roger Don't be silly. Why should your clothes be in my bathroom?

Helen That's just what *I* was thinking . . .

Sally Because I put them there, of course!

Helen In Roger's bathroom?

Sally Well, where else am I going to put them?

Helen looks at Roger, inquiringly. He cowers

Helen Roger ... ?
Roger Y-yes?
Helen Why should this lady put her clothes in your bathroom?
Sally What the hell's it got to do with you?
Roger (*to Helen*) I can explain ——!
Sally You don't have to explain anything to her!
Roger Oh, yes I do ... ! (*To Helen*) You see, Ferris made a mistake.
Ferris I knew it would be my fault.
Roger He thought Sally was sleeping in *this* room.
Ferris (*to Helen*) Yes. I did.
Sally So did I!
Roger That's why Sally put her things in here. (*Improvising, desperately*) But Ferris had forgotten all about it!
Ferris All about what?
Sally Yes, all about what?
Roger Well ... about the tap, of course!

Ferris and Sally exchange a look

Ferris ⎫
Sally ⎬ (*together*) Tap? What tap?

Roger glares at Ferris desperately

Roger The hot tap! On the basin! In the bathroom! You remember, Ferris!
Ferris No ...
Roger Yes, you do! (*He thrusts some more money into Ferris's hand*)
Ferris Yes, I do. (*To Sally*) I didn't know he meant *that* tap. (*To Roger*) You should have said.
Sally Is something wrong with it?

Ferris looks at her, blankly, for a moment

Ferris What?
Sally The hot tap! On the basin! In the bathroom!
Ferris Oh—yes! Keeps dripping. All the time. Drip, drip, drip, drip ...
Roger And he can't get a plumber till Monday.
Ferris Drip, drip, drip, drip ...
Roger And Ferris said he couldn't possibly let Sally sleep in a room with a dripping tap.
Ferris Drip, drip, drip, drip ...
Roger So Sally's going to sleep in the Blue Room.
Ferris Is she?
Sally Am I?
Helen Is she?
Roger Well, there's nobody else sleeping there!
Helen (*quietly*) I wouldn't bank on it ...
Sally So where are *you* sleeping?
Roger In here, of course!

Helen Don't you mind the dripping tap, then?

Ferris He'll have to get used to it, won't he?

Sally (*to Roger, puzzled*) You mean—*you*'re sleeping in here, and *I'm* sleeping along there?

Roger Yes! Of course!

Sally You *are* kinky, aren't you?

Roger (*to Helen, weakly*) So that's all clear, then, isn't it?

Helen I'm not sure. . . . (*She thinks hard*)

Sally It may be all clear to you, but it's not all clear to me. You still haven't told me who she is and what the hell she's doing in this room.

Roger Ah. No. I haven't, have I? (*He tries to think of a way out*) Now, let me see. . . . (*He dithers, uncertainly, then has another idea*) Good heavens! How rude of me. I'm so sorry. Didn't I introduce you? (*He indicates Helen*) This is Mrs Ferris!

Ferris glares at Roger. Sally looks astonished. Helen suppresses a giggle

Sally Mrs Ferris?

Roger Yes.

Sally His wife?

Roger Yes.

Sally (*to Ferris*) I didn't know your wife was with you.

Ferris Neither did I . . . !

Roger (*glaring at him*) Oh, come on, Ferris—surely you remember your own wife? (*He tries to push Ferris towards Helen*)

Ferris (*resisting*) No!

Roger Yes!

Ferris No!

Valiantly, Helen goes to Ferris and links her arm in his, pretending to be upset

Helen Oh, darling—have you forgotten me already?

Ferris I've never seen you before in my life!

Roger (*glaring at him*) Yes, you have!

Ferris (*defiantly*) No, I haven't!

Roger takes out a five pound note and thrusts it into Ferris's hand

Roger Yes, you have!

Ferris (*looking at the money, unimpressed*) No, I haven't . . . !

Roger glares at him and hastily gives him another note. He smiles, better pleased, and turns to Helen pretending to remember

Ah—yes—now I come to think of it—perhaps your face *is* a bit familiar. (*He chuckles*) I was only joking, darling. How could I forget you? (*He puts his arms around her*)

Sally How long have you been married, then?

Ferris } (*together*) } Six months.
Helen } { A year

Sally What?

Ferris $\left.\begin{array}{l}\\ \end{array}\right\}$ *(together)* $\left.\begin{array}{l}\\ \end{array}\right\}$ A year.
Helen Six months.

Sally You don't seem very sure.

Ferris Well, I haven't got into the swing of it, yet. (*He cuddles Helen a little*)

Sally Surely you haven't forgotten your own wedding night?

Ferris No, of course not. How could I forget that? Eh, darling? (*To Roger*) Would *you* like to hear about our wedding night, sir?

Roger (*glowering*) Well, you don't have to go into the details . . .

Ferris I'll never forget it, I can tell you. Not likely! *You* remember it, don't you, darling?

Helen Well . . . yes, I suppose so . . .

Ferris 'Course you do! (*He chuckles and puts his face close to hers*) Do you remember how I went and hid from you?

Helen (*apprehensively*) No. I don't remember that . . . !

Ferris You searched high and low, but you couldn't find me anywhere. And then—all of a sudden—I came out of the wardrobe dressed as a nun!

Helen, Sally, and Roger all look astonished

Sally Why on earth did you do that?

Ferris I thought she'd like a change of habit.

Ferris laughs at his terrible joke and looks to Roger for approval, but Roger is getting increasingly furious with him

And then—and I bet you'll never believe this—(*to Roger*) shall I tell them what happened after that, sir?

Roger No! I think we've had quite enough of your first night reminiscences, thank you, Ferris.

Ferris What a pity. I was just getting into my stride.

Roger hastily untangles Ferris from Helen

Roger Well, now you can get out of your stride and take Sally along to the Blue Room.

Ferris Why?

Roger Because that's where she's going to sleep!

Ferris I didn't know the Blue Room was empty.

Roger Well, it is!

Ferris Well that's all right then. (*To Sally*) You stick close to me, miss. (*He goes to the door*)

Sally And Roger—once I've put my things into the Blue Room, I'd like to have some dinner. *If* you can spare the time!

Sally and Ferris go out, closing the door behind them. Roger goes to embrace Helen, gratefully. Ferris returns

Ferris Now don't you go doing anything naughty with my wife.

He grins and goes out, closing the door. Roger looks at Helen, sheepishly

Roger Thanks . . .

Helen What for?

Roger For not telling her about us.

Helen Well, I didn't want to spoil your business deal, did I?

Roger Oh, good ... !

Helen Go on, then. You'd better not keep her waiting. She's obviously longing for it.

Roger Sorry?

Helen Her dinner, darling.

Roger Ah. Yes. Right. I ... I'll try not to be late, but—you know how it is ...

Roger
Helen } (*together*) Business is business!

Roger Yes ... So you'll probably be asleep when I get back.

Helen Oh, I doubt it.

Roger What?

Helen Well—that dripping tap is bound to keep me awake, isn't it? (*She smiles, enigmatically*)

Roger gives a nervous smile, kisses her briefly, and goes out, uncertain whether she is suspicious or not

Helen goes to look for her clothes, only to find they have disappeared

Helen Now where on earth have *my* clothes got to?

She goes into the bathroom

Lights out in Green Room. Ferris and Sally come down the R *stairs and go out up the* L *stairs*

Lights up in Blue Room

Geoff comes out of the bathroom, carrying his suitcase and various items of clothing. He opens his suitcase on the end of the bed, and puts everything into it, urgently. Then he goes out into the bathroom again, leaving the door ajar

As Geoff disappears, the door to the corridor opens and Ferris and Sally come in. She looks about, unimpressed

Ferris There you are, miss. What do you think of it?

Sally It's very blue. God knows what this is going to look like when I've had a few more drinks.

Ferris puts the clothes he is carrying down on the bed, and sees the open suitcase. The bathroom door shuts with a bang. Sally reacts in alarm, grabs Ferris, and they fall back on to the bed

There's someone in the bathroom!

Ferris I expect it's the plumber. (*He extricates himself*)

Sally Don't tell me this tap's dripping, as well? Anyway, I thought you couldn't get a plumber till Monday.

Ferris Ah—yes—that's right. I'd forgotten.

Sally You'd better find out who it is, and get him out of here! I do prefer a room that isn't already occupied. (*She starts to go*)

Ferris Oh—are you going?
Sally Yes. I'm going to the restaurant. I'm starving! (*She goes out, closing the door behind her*)

Geoff comes out of the bathroom, like a man in a dream

Ferris looks at him in surprise

Ferris I thought you were going.
Geoff (*miserably*) Oh, my God . . . !
Ferris What's the matter now?
Geoff (*whispering*) That voice . . .
Ferris (*whispering also*) What's wrong with my voice?
Geoff Not your voice. *That* voice.
Ferris What voice?
Geoff *Her* voice.
Ferris Her voice?
Geoff Yes. I know her voice . . .
Ferris Don't tell me you've met that lady before?
Geoff Yes! She's my wife!

Ferris cannot believe his ears. He stares at Geoff, aghast

Ferris Your *wife*?!
Geoff Yes!
Ferris (*laughing raucously*) *Your* wife staying here, as well! Oh dear, oh dear . . . ! (*He laughs even more and collapses into the armchair*)
Geoff It's nothing to laugh about. . . .
Ferris Oh, yes, it is! (*He wipes the tears away, laughing merrily*) Oh, dear. I'm sorry. I must try to control myself. (*He tries to control himself, fails and erupts into even more laughter*)
Geoff I didn't know my *wife* was staying here . . . ! (*He grabs his suitcase and makes for the door*)
Ferris Where are you going?
Geoff I'm getting out of here!
Ferris Why? Aren't you enjoying yourself?
Geoff No, I'm *not* enjoying myself! If my wife finds me here with another woman, she'll murder me. And if Roger finds me here with his wife, *he*'ll murder me! (*He opens the door*) So I'm going!
Ferris Going?
Geoff Going (*He closes the door after him*)
Ferris Gone! (*He shrugs and starts to go*)

Lights out in Blue Room

In the reception area, Sally and Roger come down opposite stairs and meet. She looks at him in mock surprise

Sally Don't tell me you're actually going to join me for dinner?
Roger (*trying to ingratiate himself*) Darling, I'm awfully sorry about the confusion.
Sally There's no confusion as far as *I*'m concerned.

Roger Isn't there? Oh, good!
Sally (*plaintively*) I just want my dinner. ...

Sally and Roger move towards the restaurant

Roger How's the new room?
Sally Very blue. I'll say one thing for you, Roger. At least you're different.
    I've never known a man take a girl away for the weekend and book *two*
    bedrooms!

Sally laughs and goes off to the restaurant

Roger is about to follow her when Geoff comes racing down the L *stairs,
carrying his suitcase*

Roger Where are *you* off to?
Geoff (*jumping a mile*) Aah! (*He turns and looks at Roger, nervously*)
Roger You don't have to go dashing off like that.
Geoff Oh yes, I do ... !
Roger But what's your girl-friend going to say when she turns up again and
    finds that her lover has packed his bag and driven off?
Geoff Well, I can't stay here! Not *now*. ...
Roger Haven't you ever done this sort of thing before?
Geoff No!!
Roger I thought not.
Geoff And I'll never do it again!
Roger Don't be daft. You'll soon get the hang of it.
Geoff No I won't! I'm going home!

Geoff runs out the main entrance just as Sally comes back from the restaurant

Sally Roger!
Roger Coming, darling.
Sally Who were you talking to?
Roger Oh, just some poor little chap who can't have what he wants.
Sally I know how he feels. Come on!

Sally drags Roger off into the restaurant

Lights up in Green Room

*Helen is on the telephone. Getting no reaction, she bangs the receiver with her
fist and the telephone in reception starts to ring as Ferris comes down the* L
stairs. He goes to answer it

Helen Is that you, Mr Ferris?
Ferris Yes, miss.
Helen This is me. Mrs Smith. I'm in Green.
Ferris I thought you were out of order, Mrs Smith.
Helen I seem to be working agan. Have you seen my clothes anywhere?
    They've disappeared.
Ferris (*defensively*) Well, *I* haven't got them! (*He is about to hang up*)
Helen Ferris ...

Ferris Yes, miss?
Helen Do you think I could have a smoked salmon sandwich?
Ferris (*outraged*) Smoked salmon?
Helen (*reasonably*) Well, I'm not having dinner.
Ferris (*reluctantly*) Oh, all right.
Helen And a glass of white wine?
Ferris (*long-suffering*) Yes, miss. (*He is about to hang up again*)
Helen And, Ferris . . .
Ferris Yes, miss?
Helen You haven't seen my Mr Smith anywhere, have you?
Ferris Oh, he's gone.
Helen (*disappointed*) Gone?
Ferris Yes. Packed his bag and went out of here as if the devil was after him.
(*He chuckles and hangs up*)

Helen hangs up, disconsolately

Helen Oh, hell! (*She puts on her sun-glasses, abruptly, and sits on the bed*)

Lights out in Green Room

Ferris is about to go when Geoff comes back, still carrying his suitcase. He looks at him in surprise

Ferris I thought you were going?
Geoff My car won't start. Where's the nearest garage?
Ferris You won't find a garage open at this time. Not around here. You'll have to stay the night, after all.
Geoff I can't do that!
Ferris You've got no choice. (*He starts to go*)
Geoff Where are you going?
Ferris To get the young lady a sandwich.
Geoff Which young lady?
Ferris *Your* young lady! The one with the glasses. (*He sighs, romantically*) She's all alone up in Green . . .
Geoff Alone?
Ferris Yes. Her husband's in the restaurant with his "client".
Geoff You said the restaurant was shut.
Ferris Well, we've opened it again! (*He starts to go*)
Geoff Can *I* have a sandwich, as well?
Ferris (*turning, abruptly*) What?
Geoff Well, I . . . I am a bit hungry.
Ferris I'm not surprised. All that dashing about. (*Conspiratorially*) Why don't you go and join her in Green? I'll bring the sarnies up there.
Geoff But what if my wife finds out?
Ferris Well, she's having dinner, isn't she?
Geoff Is she?
Ferris Yes. They're *all* having dinner! (*He laughs*)
Geoff (*tempted*) Oh—well—in that case . . .
Ferris I'll let you know if there's any danger.

Geoff Oh. Well, that's very kind of you. Here—perhaps I could—? (*He takes out his purse*)

Ferris Oh, no, sir—please!

Geoff Oh,—thank you very much. (*He is about to put his purse away*)

Ferris Well, if you insist. (*He helps himself to a few notes*) Thank you, sir!

Ferris goes out through the swing door to the kitchen

Geoff looks a little suprised, then gives an anxious glance towards the restaurant before going out up the R stairs

Lights up in Green Room. Helen is sitting on the bed with her sun-glasses on. There is a tentative knock at the door. Helen looks up. The door opens and Geoff looks in, nervously. Helen looks delighted

Helen Geoff!

Geoff Are you alone?

Helen Yes. Come on in.

Geoff comes in and closes the door

Ferris said you'd gone.

Geoff My engine won't start.

Helen I'm not surprised. I shouldn't think mine will, either. . . .

They smile at each other, a little sheepishly

I'm sorry I ran out on you. . . .

Geoff That's all right.

Helen You must have been very cross.

Geoff Well, I didn't know your husband was here then. It's bound to make a difference.

Helen Ferris is bringing me a sandwich.

Geoff I know. Me, too.

Helen (*pleased*) Are you staying here, then?

Geoff Just for a few minutes. No harm in that, is there?

They move slowly towards each other

Helen No. After all, it isn't as if anything's going to happen . . . is it?

They are about to kiss, but manage to control themselves

Geoff (*shaking his head, gloomily*) No . . .

Helen shakes her head also, but with regret

Helen No. . . .

They sit, side-by-side. Lights out in Green Room

Sally comes out of the restaurant with Roger following her, anxiously. She is now feeling the effects of her gin

Roger But, darling, they won't be very long!

She stops and turns to face him

Sally Roger, we are the only people sitting in the restaurant, and so far I haven't even seen a bread roll let alone a menu.

Roger Well, they're understaffed.

Sally They don't seem to be staffed at all! I'm going to bed! (*She starts to go*)

Roger (*following her, wheedling*) But, darling, you're all dressed up for the restaurant. . . .

Sally Well, as we're the only people in there, and you keep glancing over your shoulder, I can't think why I bothered to change! Anyway, I thought you were in a hurry to go to bed.

Roger Well . . . yes. I was.

Sally Don't tell me you've changed your mind?

Roger No, not exactly, but ——

Sally Come on, then! (*She drags him off up the* L *stairs*)

As they go, Ferris comes in through the swing door, and sees them disappearing. He reacts. He is carrying a tray on which are some smoked salmon sandwiches, two glasses and a bottle of white wine. He goes off up the R *stairs*

Lights up in Green Room. A knock at the door. Helen and Geoff leap apart, nervously, he taking her sun-glasses and hastily putting them on himself. Helen opens the door. Ferris comes in

Ferris Here we are! Smoked salmon sarnies and a bottle of dry white. (*He sets the tray down and opens the bottle*)

Geoff (*anxiously*) Have they finished yet?

Ferris Finished? The haven't even started. You've got plenty of time for it. (*He pours out two glasses of wine*)

Helen (*hopefully*) Have we?

Ferris Well, it doesn't take long to eat a smoked salmon sarnie, does it?

Ferris goes to Geoff with the bottle in one hand and a glass of wine in the other. He holds out the bottle to Geoff for his approval. Geoff takes the bottle, takes off the sun-glasses, hands them to Ferris and peers at the label on the bottle. Ferris takes a sip of wine

Geoff (*sighing, approvingly*) H'mmm . . .

Ferris (*spitting out the wine, disapprovingly*) Ugh! (*He puts on the sunglasses, takes the bottle back from Geoff and returns to the tray. He puts down the bottle and picks up the other glass of wine*)

Helen The sandwiches look delicious.

Ferris Thank you, miss.

Helen takes her sun-glasses back from Ferris

Helen Thank you, Ferris.

Ferris, temporarily blinded by the sudden light, turns and nearly walks into the door with the two glasses of wine

Thank you, Ferris!

Ferris (*realizing, turns*) Ah! Thank *you*, miss.

Ferris hands the two glasses of wine to Helen, laughs and stumbles out, closing the door behind him

Helen hands one glass of wine to Geoff. Then she goes and sits in the armchair. They look at each other, shyly

Helen Well—cheers . . .
Geoff Yes—cheers . . .

They raise their glasses. Lights crossfade from Green Room to Blue Room

The door opens and Sally comes in, followed by Roger. The gin has now definitely caught up with her. He looks about at the blue walls and shudders

Roger Oh, my God. That *is* blue.
Sally Well, I'll have to keep your mind off it, won't I?
Roger What?

She smiles, kicks off her shoes, lies down on the bed and looks up at the ceiling

   What are you doing?
Sally I'm lying down on the bed. I've had no food and lots of gin.
Roger (*hovering, nervously*) I really think we ought to go back to the restaurant.
Sally Don't be such a spoilsport. Come here.
Roger I'll ring for a sandwich.
Sally I don't want a sandwich!
Roger Well, I do. I'm hungry.
Sally Come over here . . . !
Roger No!
Sally You were so keen before. . . .
Roger Well, it's different now.
Sally (*calling*) Champagne!
Roger What?
Sally I want champagne! You promised me champagne . . . !

Roger tries to quieten Sally casting an anxious look towards the door

Roger All right! All right! I'll get champagne. (*He starts to go*)
Sally You don't have to go downstairs.
Roger Yes, I do!
Sally Ferris said he'd bring champagne the moment he heard us banging on the floor. . . .
Roger (*fearfully*) Oh, my God, so he did. . . . !
Sally So—come on! (*She gets up, unsteadily, and takes him by the hand*) Let's bang on the floor together. . . . ! (*She starts to jump up and down on the floor, laughing*)

He casts another anxious look towards the door, and joins in, nervously

   One—two—three—four . . . !

Ferris comes down the R *stairs. He hears the banging, and reacts*

Ferris *Now* what the hell are they up to?

Ferris runs out up the L *stairs*

Sally and Roger are still jumping up and down on the floor: she, happily; he, miserably

The door opens and Ferris comes in and sees them. He cannot believe his eyes. He takes a small whistle out of his pocket and blows a sharp blast. Sally and Roger stop bouncing, and see him

Ferris Now, look here—my sister doesn't allow morris dancing. Not in the bedrooms.

Sally goes, unsteadily, to Ferris and peers at him, accusingly

Sally You haven't got any!

Ferris does not know what she means

Ferris I beg your pardon?
Sally We were banging on the floor for champagne.
Ferris I wondered what you were doing.
Sally Champagne ... ! I need champagne. . . . (*She wanders away and sinks on to the bed again*)
Roger You'll have to get champagne.
Ferris I'll see what I can do, sir.
Sally (*dreamily*) I want champagne ... (*And with that she collapses back on to the bed and is silent*)

Roger and Ferris peer at her, then, satisfied that she is asleep, Roger takes Ferris away a little and speaks quietly

Roger Is my wife still in Green?
Ferris Oh, yes. She's settled down *very* nicely. Smoked salmon sarnies and white wine.
Roger (*a little put out*) Smoked salmon and white wine?
Ferris Yes.
Roger She's not likely to start looking for me, then?
Ferris Oh, no. I think she's got everything she wants at the moment.
Sally (*sleepily*) Champagne. . . . When shall I see champagne ... ?

Ferris and Roger exchange a look

Ferris You sure you can manage on your own, sir?
Roger What?
Ferris Well, if she's like this now, what's she going to be like after champagne?

Ferris goes, closing the door behind him

Roger tiptoes back to Sally. She is lying still. He thinks she may be asleep and bends over her to make sure

Roger (*whispering*) Sally. . . . Are you asleep?

*Roger looks pleased, and is about to leave when she grabs him and pulls him
down on top of her, giggling happily. Lights out in Blue Room*

> *Ferris comes down the L stairs and goes out through the swing door to the
> kitchen*

*Lights up in Green Room. Helen and Geoff have finished their sandwiches and
are sipping the wine, contentedly*

Helen H'm. I love smoked salmon.
Geoff So do I. . . .

A pause

Helen Do you know what I want now?
Geoff Er . . . no. (*But he moves a little closer*)
Helen Chocolate! I'm going to have a chocolate. (*She gets up to look for
them*)
Geoff The way you were going at them, I shouldn't think there are any left.
Helen Now, where did I put them? (*She remembers*) Of course! (*She starts to
go*)
Geoff *Now* where are you going?
Helen I left them in the Blue Room!

She puts on her sun-glasses and goes, closing the door behind her

*Geoff sighs, unhappily, and sits down again. Lights crossfade from Green
Room to Blue Room*

*Sally and Roger are struggling on the bed. He manages to escape, but she
follows him, giggling*

Sally Don't be such a spoilsport!
Roger Ferris'll be back in a minute!
Sally Lock the door, then. He can leave the champagne outside.
Roger No! Not now!

Sally closes with him and tries to embrace him. He resists, manfully

*Helen comes down the R stairs with her sun-glasses on, and goes off up the L
stairs*

Roger Go away! Please! You must go away!
Sally I thought this was what we came here to do?
Roger Yes. It was. But I'm not in the mood now.
Sally (*giggling*) Oh, go on—get your trousers off!
Roger What?!
Sally Well, you can't go to bed with your trousers on, can you? Oh, come
on, darling . . .
Roger (*giving in, reluctantly*) Oh, all right. But only for a minute.

*She laughs at him as he looks around, nervously, then unzips his trousers. He
gets them down to below his knees before good sense prevails*

No! I mustn't! (*He starts to pull them up again*)
Sally Yes, you must!

She pushes him and he falls backwards onto the bed. She grabs the ends of his trousers and pulls them off him, holding them up in the air, triumphantly. Roger is wearing colourful jockey shorts

Eureka!

A knock at the door. Roger leaps up and hovers, terrified

Helen (*off*) Is anybody there?
Roger Oh, my God! (*He dives for cover under the duvet*)
Sally Whatever's the matter? It's only Mrs Ferris.

She starts to get under the duvet with him, so he leaps out and escapes from her

Roger (*whispering, desperately*) Give me back my trousers!
Sally (*with a big smile*) No. You come and get them.
Helen Is anybody there?
Roger Oh, no ... !

He races out into the bathroom and closes the door

Sally laughs at his discomfort. She throws the trousers over the end of the bed as the door opens and Helen comes in

Helen Oh. Sorry. Nobody answered, so I thought you were still having dinner.
Sally I got tired of waiting to be served. So I'm going to bed.
Helen Oh. Have you *finished* your business, then?
Sally We haven't even started! (*She sits on the bed, giggling*)

Ferris comes through the swing door, carrying a tray on which is a bottle of champagne and two glasses. He goes off up the L stairs

Helen I won't disturb you. I just came to get my chocolates. (*She notices the trousers on the end of the bed*) Did you know that there's a pair of gentleman's trousers on the end of your bed?
Sally Yes. He left them behind. (*She giggles*)
Helen Who did?

Roger knocks something over in the bathroom. Helen looks towards the noise

Is somebody in the bathroom?
Sally (*smiling, happily*) Yes! He's hiding. Isn't it exciting? (*She lies back, laughing*)

The bedroom door opens and Ferris walks in. He stops when he sees Helen there instead of Roger

Ferris (*unhappily*) Oh, no! What are you doing in Blue? I left you in Green!
Helen I came to get my chocolates.

Ferris glances at Sally lying on the bed, and speaks aside to Helen

Ferris Was anyone *else* here when you arrived?

Helen Only her.

Ferris Thank heaven for that ... !

Sally (*impatiently*) Ferris—will you please open the bloody champagne!

Ferris Oh. Yes. Right. (*He starts to open it, but in the middle he spots the trousers on the end of the bed and peers at them*) Oh, my good Lord. . . . ! (*He hides his face in his hands for a moment*)

Sally What's the matter?

Ferris There's a pair of gentleman's trousers on the end of your bed. You've had a man in here taking his trousers off, haven't you?

Sally (*smiling, happily*) Yes, I have!

Ferris I thought so ... ! (*The champagne pops and he pours a glass for Sally*)

Helen is peering through her sun-glasses at the trousers

Helen You know—I think I've seen those trousers somewhere before. ... (*She lifts her glasses a little to get a better look*)

Ferris No, you haven't!

He puts down the bottle of champagne, picks up the trousers and throws them to Sally, who throws them back to him

You've never seen them before in your life!

He throws them to Sally, who again throws them back to him, giggling

Helen I'm sure I have. Let me take a look.

Ferris peers, briefly, into the trousers, unimpressed

Ferris No! They're just ordinary trousers! (*As he speaks, he turns them inside out*) Nothing special about them. You don't want to look at ordinary trousers, do you?

Helen Yes, I do!

Ferris They're the sort of trousers you can see anywhere. Common trousers. Very common. There's no point in looking at common trousers. (*To Sally*) Did the occupant of these common trousers say where he was going?

Sally Well, he wasn't going far without his trousers, was he? (*She laughs*)

Helen He's in the bathroom.

Ferris What?!

Helen Yes. She's got somebody hidden in the bathroom.

Ferris (*looking at Sally in hopeful disbelief*) You haven't!

Sally I have ... ! He got shy and hid in there when Helen arrived.

Ferris I'm not surprised ... !

Sally (*getting off the bed*) I'll tell him he can come out now.

Ferris No!!

But Sally has gone into the bathroom

Ferris turns to Helen, desperately, and tries to urge her on her way

Come on! You can't stay here!

Helen Why not?

Ferris You don't want to see her Mr Smith coming out of the bathroom without his trousers!

Helen Oh, yes, I do . . . !

Sally comes out of the bathroom, looking rather puzzled

Sally How extraordinary. . . .

Helen What?

Sally He's disappeared!

Helen What?

Sally There's no sign of him.

Ferris (*quietly*) Thank God for that! I was starting to get another of my headaches . . .

Sally He must have climbed out of the window.

Helen But if he's climbed out of the window, where will he have gone to?

Ferris *I* know where he'll have gone to . . . ! (*He goes, quickly, to the door*)

Sally Where are you off to?

Ferris I'm going to see to the dirty linen.

He goes, closing the door behind him

Sally and Helen look at each other in surprise

Lights crossfade from Blue Room to Green Room. Geoff is sipping his wine, contentedly. He looks up as the bathroom door opens

> *Roger comes in, without his trousers but with his jacket still on. The two men gaze at each other, blankly, for a while. Roger fastens his jacket and tries to appear nonchalant. Finally . . .*

Roger What the hell are you doing in my bedroom?

Geoff What?

Roger I thought you'd gone home.

Geoff My car won't start.

Roger That's no reason for being in my bedroom.

Geoff I—I was helping Ferris with the room service. (*He hastily puts the glasses and plates on to the tray*) They're very short-staffed. I didn't know you were in the bathroom.

Roger I wasn't. I've just arrived.

Geoff In the bathroom?

Roger Yes.

Geoff How did you *get* into the bathroom?

Roger Through the window.

Geoff Is that how you lost your trousers?

Roger looks down at his bare legs, as if seeing them for the first time

Roger Ah. No. I'd lost them before.

Geoff (*appalled*) Not in the restaurant!

Roger No, no! In the Blue Room.

Geoff That's *my* room!

Roger Not any more. You went home and left it empty.

Geoff And you went in and took your trousers off?

Roger Yes.

Geoff (*realizing*) Ah! With your . . . ?

Roger Client. Yes. But then my wife arrived, looking for chocolate.

Geoff You must have had a bit of a shock.

Roger I did! So I climbed out of the blue bathroom window and came along here.

Geoff Does Helen know that you're in the blue bathroom?

Roger She knows *somebody* is.

Ferris races down the L stairs, gathers his breath, and then races out up the R stairs

    I say! This *is* a bit of luck!

Geoff What is?

Roger You being here. You're just the man I need. Get your trousers off.

Geoff What?!

Roger Your trousers. Get 'em off.

Geoff starts to undo his trousers, then stops

Geoff What for?

Roger Look—if my wife finds me in that other bathroom, there'll be hell to pay.

Geoff There certainly will!

Roger But if *you* walk out of the bathroom, that'll be all right.

Geoff (*not so sure*) Will it?

Roger Well, it was your room! So Helen will think that *my* girl-friend is *your* girl-friend. And that'll put *me* in the clear.

Geoff Yes. But where will it put *me*?

Roger (*impatiently*) Well, it can't matter to you if my wife finds you with another woman, can it?

Geoff (*hastily*) Ah—no—no, of course not!

Roger Well, come on, then—get 'em off!

Geoff (*puzzled*) But why do I have to take my trousers off?

Roger Because you're pretending to be the one in the blue bathroom, and he left his trousers in the blue bedroom. So come on—hurry up! Get 'em off!

Geoff No! No—I won't do it! (*He clings on to his trousers*)

Roger tickles him under the arms, making him leave go of his trousers. They struggle and Geoff's trousers are removed, revealing long colourful shorts

Whereupon, Ferris walks in, and is astonished to see two men on the bed, grappling with each other with their trousers off. He takes out his whistle and blows a long blast. Roger and Geoff see him

Ferris Is this a private party or can *anyone* join in?

Roger I'm helping him off with his trousers.

Ferris Yes. I could see that.

Roger He's giving me a hand.

Ferris I wondered what he was doing. How did you get in here?

Roger Through the window.

Ferris Like Peter Pan.

Roger (*to Geoff, impatiently*) Come on, Geoff! Off you go!

Ferris Where's he going without his trousers?

Roger To the blue bathroom.

Ferris Why?

Roger Because I don't want my wife to find *me* in another woman's bathroom.

Ferris (*fearfully*) You mean your wife—and your girl-friend—are going to find *him* in the bathroom instead?

Roger Of course!

Ferris No, they mustn't do that!

Roger Why not? What difference does it make who my wife finds in the blue bathroom as long as it isn't me?

Ferris (*quietly*) It's not *your* wife I'm worried about ... !

Roger Come on, Geoff! Don't hang about. It's perfectly simple. You go out of the window, along the little ledge ——

Geoff (*alarmed*) What?

Roger There's a little ledge outside. You can crawl along that.

Geoff (*appalled*) A little ledge!

Roger Well, *I* did it.

Geoff Yes, but you were in trouble.

Ferris So will you be if you go along there ... !

Geoff But when your girlfriend opens the bathroom door, expecting to see you, and sees *me* instead, isn't she going to be rather surprised?

Ferris (*quietly*) Yes, so are you ... !

Roger Look, don't you *want* to help me?

Geoff (*doubtfully*) Well—yes—I suppose so—but—

Roger Get on with it, then! There's no time to discuss it. Off you go!

Ferris No—he mustn't!

But it is too late. Roger pushes the reluctant Geoff out into the bathroom, and shuts the door

Roger Honestly, the fuss some people make. (*He picks up Geoff's trousers*)

Ferris (*wearily*) How long does it take to get along to the other bathroom?

Roger About two minutes.

Ferris Oh, my God—here I go again ... !

Ferris races out

Roger watches him go, surprised, and then takes Geoff's trousers out into the bathroom

Lights out in Green Room. Ferris races down the R stairs, gathers his breath, and races off up the L stairs

Lights up in Blue Room. Sally is sipping champagne, serenely. Helen is turning Roger's trousers the right way out. She stares at them, grimly

Helen I thought so!

Sally What?

Helen These belong to my husband!

Sally Don't be silly. They belong to Roger.

Helen (*seething*) *Roger*? So it *was* Roger in the bathroom?

Sally Well, who did you think it was?

Helen rolls up the trousers into an angry ball and throws them at Sally, who catches them and stares at Helen, astonished

Sally Have you gone mad? You've crushed Roger's trousers.

Helen I shall crush more than his trousers when I get hold of him!

Sally I don't know what you're making such a fuss about. He's not *your* husband.

Helen Oh, yes, he is!

Sally (*appalled*) I thought you were married to Ferris!

Helen Well, I'm not!

Sally Oh, my God ... !

Helen begins to roar, like a small, angry lion, and advances on Sally

Don't you come near me!

She tries to escape, but Helen grabs her and they fall on to the bed in a struggling heap

Whereupon, Ferris comes in and sees them. He looks astonished, takes out his whistle and blows a sharp blast. Helen and Sally sort themselves out

Ferris What on earth are you doing?

Helen I'm reclaiming my husband's property. (*She holds the trousers aloft*)

Ferris Don't be silly—*I'm* your husband! (*He grabs the trousers and starts to put them on over his own*)

Helen Not any more!

Ferris (*stopping*) What?

Sally Those belong to her *real* husband.

Ferris takes the trousers off and stares at them in overdone surprise

Ferris Good heavens! How did *his* trousers get in here?

Helen You needn't bother, Ferris. I know all about it.

Ferris You do?

Sally Ferris! You said this lady ——

Ferris There's no time for explanations! (*He starts picking up her clothes and thrusting them into her arms*) You've got to get out of here!

Sally Why?

Ferris Because you're in the wrong room.

Sally You told me this was the *right* room.

Ferris Well, it's not! It's the wrong room!

He drags her out, closing the door behind them

The moment the door has closed, the bathroom door opens and Geoff comes in, without his trousers but with his jacket still on

Helen gazes at him, astonished. He is deeply embarrassed and shifts, uncomfortably. He fastens his jacket and tries to appear nonchalant. Finally ...

Helen What on earth are you doing in here?
Geoff I ... I'm coming out of the bathroom.
Helen Without your trousers?
Geoff Ah. Yes. Well ...
Helen How did you get *into* the bathroom?
Geoff There's a little ledge. Outside. All along the ... Oh, dear! (*He shudders at the memory*)
Helen (*concerned for him*) You might have fallen off!
Geoff I very nearly did.
Helen But why did you do it?
Geoff (*blankly*) What?
Helen You don't usually crawl along little ledges in the middle of the night.
Geoff No. I've never done it before.
Helen (*smiling*) And you needn't have done it now.
Geoff Sorry?
Helen I *know* it was Roger in the bathroom.
Geoff You do?
Helen *And* I know all about him and his ... "client".
Geoff You do?
Helen Yes.
Geoff Oh. I don't think he knows that. I'm very sorry.
Helen (*cheerfully*) There's nothing to be sorry about.
Geoff No?
Helen No.
Geoff Oh.
Helen After all, now it doesn't matter if Roger finds out about *us*, does it?
Geoff (*alarmed*) What?
Helen So let's get on with it. (*She sits him down in the armchair*)
Geoff Get on with it?
Helen (*smiling reasonably*) Well, you have got your trousers off, haven't you?

He looks down at his bare legs. She sits on his knee. Lights out in Blue Room

Ferris comes down the L stairs, leading Sally by the hand. She is still laden with her clothes and is grumbling

Sally I wish you'd make up your mind which room I'm supposed to be in. I feel like a wandering gypsy.
Ferris You wouldn't have liked that room, miss. It's far too blue.
Sally But we left the champagne behind! (*She tries to go back*)
Ferris Never mind the champagne. Come on! (*He drags her off up the R stairs*)

Lights up in Green Room. Roger comes in from the bathroom in Geoff's trousers, which are far too short for him

The door opens and Ferris comes in with Sally. She looks at him in surprise

Sally You disappeared!

Roger I had no choice.

Sally How did you get back here?

Roger There's a little ledge. Outside. All along the ... Oh, dear! (*He shudders at the memory*) I might have fallen off.

Sally (*livid*) I wish you had!

Roger What?

Sally Why didn't you tell me that Helen was your wife?

Roger I didn't know.

Sally Didn't know?!

Roger Didn't want you to know. (*He turns to Ferris*) It's all your fault!

Ferris Yes, I thought it would be ...

Sally What's she *doing* here, anyway?

Roger Who?

Sally Your wife!

Roger I've no idea. Anyway, what are *you* doing here? You're supposed to be in the Blue Room.

Sally I seem to be moving back in with you.

Roger Oh, no, you're not! (*To Ferris*) Why have you brought her back here?

Ferris Because the Blue Room's getting rather crowded!

Sally starts to laugh, pointing at Roger's short trousers, fascinated

Sally Where on earth did you get those trousers?

Roger What? (*He looks down at them*) Oh—these! Yes. Not much of a fit, I'm afraid. (*He tries to make his short trousers appear a little more presentable*)

Sally watches, hysterical

Sally Is that how they came back from the cleaners?

Ferris looks apprehensive

Roger No—no, of course not! I—I borrowed them from a friend.

Ferris Oh, God ... !

Sally (*suddenly looking puzzled*) Wait a minute. ... (*She leans forward, peering at the offending trousers*) I think I've seen those trousers somewhere before ...

She tries to get a better look. Ferris hastily gets between them and extemporizes a dance to distract Sally from the trousers

Ferris No! You haven't! You've never seen them before in your life!

Sally I'm sure I have. (*Thoughtfully*) I think I know someone who wears trousers just like those ... Do get out of the way, Ferris! I want to have a look.

Ferris stays close to Roger, like a limpet. Roger does not know what Ferris is making such a fuss about

Ferris No! No—you mustn't see them!

Roger Ferris! What's the matter with you? She can look at them if she wants to.

Ferris No, she can't!

Roger Why not?

Sally Do get out of the way, Ferris ...

Ferris You don't want to see these trousers. They're very ordinary trousers.

Sally (*giggling*) They're very *short* trousers.

Ferris Yes—ordinary short trousers! You don't want to look at ordinary short trousers.

Sally Yes, I do!

Ferris No, you don't!

Sally Whatever's the matter with you?

Ferris whispers over his shoulder to Roger, urgently

Ferris Get them off!

Roger (*astonished*) What?

Ferris Get 'em off, sir!

Roger Have you gone mad?

Ferris Very probably. (*Desperately*) Trust me, sir—and get 'em off!

Totally bewildered, but wary of Ferris's urgency, Roger starts to take off his trousers with Ferris forming a human screen. Sally watches, unable to believe her eyes, trying to control her mirth. Roger hands the short trousers to Ferris

Roger There you are, Ferris.

Ferris Thank you, sir. (*He rolls the trousers up into a ball*) I'll go and get your other pair. (*He makes for the door*)

Roger Good idea!

Sally Where are you going with those trousers?

Ferris I'm going to look for a short man with bare legs.

Ferris goes, quickly, closing the door behind him

Sally and Roger look at each other. Lights out in Green Room

Ferris comes staggering down the R stairs, gathers his breath, and races out up the L stairs

Lights up in Blue Room. Helen and Geoff are as before. She takes his hand and leads him, purposefully, towards the bed

Helen Come on, darling! Don't let's waste any more time.

Geoff But what if your husband comes back and finds us?

Helen I don't care if he does now I know what *he's* been up to! (*She advances*)

Geoff (*backing, nervously*) No! Not now! Not in here!

Helen Oh, come on, Geoff! Don't be such a spoilsport. (*She grabs him and they fall on to the bed*)

Whereupon, Ferris comes in and sees another assorted couple rolling on a bed! He takes out his whistle and blows a sharp blast. Helen and Geoff leap apart and hastily sort themselves out; he embarrassed, she annoyed at the interruption

Helen What do you want, Ferris?

Ferris I'm looking for a short man without his trousers. (*He peers at Geoff*) I think that must be you, sir. (*He goes towards him*)

Geoff (*rather cross*) I don't need my trousers up here!

Ferris I can see that! But I thought it might be safer.

Geoff Safer?

Ferris closes to him, confidentially

Ferris There was a lady looking at them.

Geoff (*alarmed*) Not *that* lady?

Ferris I'm afraid so.

Geoff She saw my trousers?!

Ferris I think so.

Geoff grabs his trousers from Ferris and starts to put them on

Helen (*puzzled*) What does it matter if some strange lady saw your trousers?

Geoff (*to Ferris*) How did she react?

Ferris Not very well, sir!

Helen Why should a strange lady be interested in your trousers?

Ferris I think she was wondering how they came to be here.

Geoff Where is she now?

Ferris Depends if she's realized or not.

Geoff And if she *has*?

Ferris She'll be on her way up here.

Geoff Oh, my God ... ! (*He heads for the bathroom*)

Helen Where are you going?

Geoff Well, I can't stay here! Can I, Ferris?

Ferris I wouldn't recommend it.

Geoff I'll have to go this way.

Helen (*appalled*) Back along the little ledge?

Geoff Well, I've got my trousers on.

Helen Won't you be frightened?

Geoff I'll be more frightened if I stay here!

He scuttles out into the bathroom and shuts the door

Helen I can't think why he's so upset about someone seeing his trousers ...

Ferris (*quietly*) *I* can ... ! (*He realizes something*) Wait a minute ...

Helen What's the matter?

Ferris If he goes back along the little ledge ... he'll end up in the other bathroom.

Helen (*calmly*) Yes. Of course he will.

Ferris (*wearily*) Oh, my God—here I go again ... !

He picks up Roger's trousers and races out, closing the door behind him. Helen looks puzzled, collects her box of chocolates and goes out. Lights out in Blue Room

Ferris comes racing down the L stairs, stops to catch his breath, and races off up the R stairs

Lights up in Green Room. Sally is locking the door. Roger looks apprehensive

Roger What are you doing?
Sally Locking the door, of course. We don't want to waste any more time, do we?
Roger What?
Sally Well darling—you have got your trousers off . . .

She closes to him, seductively. He escapes from her and moves away

Roger You keep away from me! I'm in enough trouble already. (*Like a small, angry child*) Give me the key! I want to get my trousers!
Sally Come and get it, then. (*She puts the key inside her bra, and smiles at him, enjoying his discomfort*)
Roger No fear! (*He heads for the bathroom*)
Sally Where are you going?
Roger If you won't give me the key I'm going back the way I came!
Sally Along the little ledge?
Roger Yes!

He goes, shutting the bathroom door with a bang

An urgent rattle at the other door as someone tries to get in. Sally goes and unlocks it. Ferris bustles in, carrying Roger's trousers

Ferris Come on—get your things! (*He picks up her clothes again and dumps them in her arms*)
Sally What are you doing?
Ferris You can't stay here!
Sally Why not?
Ferris You're in the wrong room.
Sally You said this was the right room!
Ferris I was wrong. It's the wrong room. Go back to Blue. Do not pass "Go". Do not collect two hundred pounds.

He pushes her out into the corridor with her clothes, then races across to the bathroom with Roger's trousers

Mr Smith! (*He opens the bathroom door and looks in*) Are you in there, Mr Smith? (*He comes out and slams the door shut*) Now where the hell's *he* got to?

He races out of the door to the corridor, closing it behind him with a bang. Lights out in Green Room

Sally comes down the R stairs. At the same time, Helen comes down the L stairs with her box of chocolates. They meet, face-to-face. Sally looks somewhat apprehensive

Sally Don't you come near me . . . !

But Helen smiles happily, and offers her chocolates to Sally

Helen Would you like to have a chocolate?
Sally (*smiling, relieved*) Why not? It's the only thing I *am* going to have tonight.

She takes a chocolate, and they both laugh. Helen takes a chocolate, too

Ferris comes down the R *stairs and goes to Sally*

Ferris (*urgently*) Where is he?
Sally Who?
Ferris Your Mr Smith!
Sally (*calmly*) He went out of the bathroom window again.
Helen So did *my* Mr Smith!
Sally (*puzzled*) I didn't know you'd got a Mr Smith.
Ferris Of course she's got a Mr Smith! What do you think she came to *this* place for?
Sally (*to Helen, smiling delightedly*) You mean *you* came here for the same thing that *I* did?
Helen Yes!

They both laugh, cosily, all girls together

Ferris So *your* Mr Smith and *your* Mr Smith have both gone out of the bathroom window?
Sally }
Helen } (*together*) Yes!
Ferris (*laughing, noisily*) I bet they never thought they'd be spending the night perched on a ledge like a couple of seagulls!

Roger comes in from the main entrance. He is still without his trousers, is somewhat dishevelled, and has a few twigs from a tree clinging to him here and there

They all stare at him in surprise

Roger Have you seen my wife anywhere?
Helen Roger!

He sees her and overdoes his reaction somewhat

Roger Hullo, darling!
Helen (*coldly*) Never mind "Hullo, darling"! What have you been doing?
Roger I've been looking for you.
Helen Well, you wouldn't find me outside the bathroom window!
Roger Ah—there was a good reason for that.
Helen Was there a good reason for taking your trousers off, as well?
Roger I can explain ——!
Ferris Your trousers, sir.
Roger Oh, thank you, Ferris. I wondered where they'd got to. (*He takes the trousers from Ferris and starts to put them on*)
Ferris Whatever happened?

Roger That bloody fool was out there on the little ledge, as well! And he tried to get past me! Lucky for us there was a tree underneath.
Ferris You mean both Mr Smiths fell off?
Roger Yes!

Ferris laughs, noisily

(*Glaring at him*) It's not funny, Ferris!
Ferris Oh, yes, it is—here comes the other one!

Geoff comes unsteadily into view from the main entrance. Like Roger, he is dishevelled and wearing a few twigs. A small bird's nest has attached itself to the back of his neck

They watch in surprise as he approaches. Especially Sally, who is seeing him for the first time in the play and cannot believe her eyes! Geoff crosses, miserably, to Sally

Geoff H-h-hullo ...
Sally (*to Helen, intrigued*) Is *this* the other Mr Smith?

Geoff looks alarmed, but Helen, unaware of the situation, smiles at Sally and nods, innocently

Helen Yes!
Sally (*turning to Geoff again*) Geoffrey, darling—what a *lovely* surprise! And I didn't even know that you were staying here.

Roger and Helen look puzzled

Roger Do you two know each other, then?
Sally Know each other? We're married!

Roger and Helen look aghast

Roger Oh, my God ...! (*Turning to Ferris, furiously*) You never told me that!
Ferris I didn't think you'd want to know ...!
Helen (*to Sally, in disbelief*) He's ... your *husband*?
Sally Yes! *Isn't* that a coincidence?
Helen We'd better have another chocolate!

Sally and Helen laugh together, enjoying the funny side, and help themselves to chocolates. Roger and Geoff are bewildered

Roger I don't know what *they*'re laughing about.
Ferris *I* do ...! (*And he laughs, also*)
Sally Geoffrey, darling—where have you hidden your girl-friend? I can't wait to see her ...

Sally and Helen giggle together

Geoff W-what?
Roger Yes—whatever happened to her? She never turned up again, did she?
Geoff (*nervously*) Ah—no—well ...

Ferris (*helpfully*) Oh, she *left*, didn't she, sir?
Geoff Did she?

Ferris nods, encouragingly

Ah—yes! Thank you, Ferris.
Ferris Thank *you*, sir. (*He holds out his hand*)

Geoff reacts to the outstretched hand and hastily gives some money to Ferris, who smiles, gratefully

Geoff (*to Roger*) Yes—she left. Had to go home.
Roger You said her car was still outside.
Geoff D-did I?
Ferris (*whispering, urgently*) Taxi!
Geoff Taxi! Thank you, Ferris.
Ferris Thank *you*, sir. (*He holds out his hand again*)

Geoff looks displeased, but gives Ferris another note. Ferris nods, contentedly

Geoff (*to Sally*) Yes—she took a taxi. I remember now.
Helen And where have you hidden *your* girl-friend, Roger? *She* doesn't seem to be here, either.

Helen and Sally giggle together

Geoff (*going to Roger, astonished*) Does your wife *know* about your—?
Roger Yes!
Geoff So we're both in the same boat?
Ferris Yes! In more ways than one! (*He laughs, raucously*)
Sally Don't tell me your girl-friend has disappeared, as well, Roger?
Roger (*quietly*) I wish she had ... !
Geoff (*helpfully*) Perhaps she's still in the restaurant.
Ferris Yes—looking for nuts ... !
Helen (*to Sally*) Let's go and find her, shall we?

They start to go. Roger goes quickly to them

Roger No! No—she's not there anymore!
Helen Then where is she?
Ferris (*quietly*) Didn't *she* leave, as well, sir?
Roger Did she?
Ferris You remember! Her mother was taken ill!
Roger Ah—yes! Of course! Thank you, Ferris!
Ferris Thank *you*, sir. (*He holds out his hand*)

Roger quickly hands over some money. Ferris pockets it, gratefully. Roger turns to Helen again, smiling happily

Roger Yes—that's right—her mother was taken ill, so she left! (*He escapes, triumphantly, back to Geoff*)
Sally (*in mock sympathy*) Oh—and she never got her dinner ...

Sally and Helen giggle together

Geoff (*to Roger*) So *both* our girl-friends have disappeared?
Roger Yes. (*Thoughtfully*) Quite a coincidence ...

Roger and Geoff consider this, deeply

Ferris turns to the girls, smiling happily

Ferris Well, now that's all settled let's open some more champagne!
Sally }(*together*) Good idea!
Helen

Ferris and the girls start to go

Roger Just a minute!

Ferris and the girls stop and look back at Roger, innocently

Ferris Yes, sir?
Roger There's something I don't understand ...
Ferris *Really*, sir?
Geoff There's something *I* don't understand, either. ...
Ferris Oh, surely not, sir?
Roger What was my wife doing staying all by herself in a deserted hotel in the depths of the country?
Geoff And what was *my* wife doing here, too?
Ferris I wouldn't ask them that, if I were you!
Roger Why not?
Ferris Well, what sort of a question would that be for a man to ask his own wife? Don't tell me you two don't trust your own wives?

Roger and Geoff look suitably shame-faced and go to their wives. Sally and Helen try to control their giggles

Roger Well ... yes—of course we do!
Geoff Yes—naturally ... !
Ferris And so I should think! So let's hear no more about it. I should take them upstairs while you've still got the chance.

Helen } (*together to their*   Good idea!
Sally } *respective husbands*) Come along, darling!

The girls start to drag their bewildered husbands towards the stairs

Ferris I'll be up in a minute.

The couples stop and look back at him in surprise

Roger
Sally
Geoff } (*together*) What?!
Helen
Ferris } With the champagne! And don't you start without me!

The music swells and Ferris is scuttling out into the kitchen and the girls are dragging their husbands upstairs, smiling happily, as ——

the CURTAIN *falls*

It rises again immediately and the two couples come down the staircases and take their bows. Only once more Roger is with Sally, and Geoff with Helen! Ferris comes through the swing door carrying two large bottles of champagne, one with a blue ribbon and one with a green. He takes his bow. Then he notices the wrongly-assorted couples and goes, hastily, to move Sally across to Geoff, and Helen across to Roger, giving each couple a bottle of champagne. The couples embrace and Ferris smiles, happily, having sorted them out at last

the CURTAIN *falls*

FURNITURE AND PROPERTY LIST

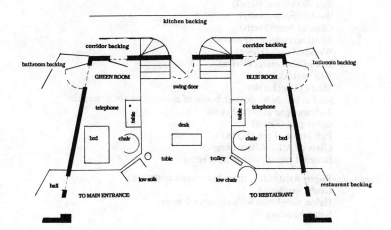

kitchen backing

corridor backing | corridor backing

bathroom backing | GREEN ROOM | BLUE ROOM | bathroom backing

swing door

telephone | telephone

table | table

desk

bed | chair | chair | bed

table | trolley

low sofa | low chair

hall | restaurant backing

TO MAIN ENTRANCE | TO RESTAURANT

ACT I

On stage: *In reception*:
Reception desk. *On it*: bell, telephone, pencil fastened to desk by string,
paperweight. *In it*: notepad, piece of soap, hotel register (with dust)
Drinks trolley. *On it*: bottle of gin (nearly finished), bottle of whisky,
bottles of tonic water, glasses, small tray, dish of nuts
Low-backed chair
Small sofa
Coffee table

In Blue Room:
Bed *On it*: bedding including a duvet
Table. *On it*: telephone, ashtray
Small armchair
Shoes **(Geoff)**
Key in door

In Green Room:
Bed *On it*: bedding including a duvet
Table
Small armchair
Shoes **(Roger)**
Jacket **(Roger)**
Key in door

Off stage: Toothbrush **(Roger)**
           Glass of water **(Roger)**
           Eau de cologne **(Roger)**
           Sandwich **(Ferris)**
           'Daily Mirror' **(Ferris)**
           Toothbrush **(Geoff)**
           Glass of water **(Geoff)**
           Eau de cologne **(Geoff)**
           Weekend case **(Sally)**
           Glass of beer **(Ferris)**
           Small screwdriver **(Ferris)**
           Weekend case **(Helen)**
           Box of chocolates **(Helen)**
           Nail varnish **(Sally)**
           Mug of tea **(Ferris)**
           Ice bucket. *In it*: quarter bottle of champagne *On it:* napkin
           2 champagne glasses **(Ferris)**
           Order pad **(Ferris)**
           Full bottle of gin **(Ferris)**
           Glass of Alka-Seltzer **(Roger)**
           Battered menu (*with dust*) **(Ferris)**

Personal: **Roger:** wristwatch, three five-pound notes, coins
          Geoff: wristwatch
          Helen: sunglasses with coloured frames
          Sally: handbag

ACT II

Check: Dust on telephone in reception

Off-stage Empty glass **(Sally)**
          Suitcase **(Geoff)**
          Tray. *On it*: bottle of white wine, two glasses, two sandwiches, two plates
            (Ferris)
          Tray. *On it*: bottle of champagne, two glasses **(Ferris)**
          Twigs, bits of ivy, etc. **(Roger)**
          Twigs, bird's nest, etc. **(Geoff)**
          Two large champagne bottles, one with a blue ribbon and the other with a
            green one **(Ferris)**

Personal **Ferris:** whistle
         Roger: number of five-pound notes
         Geoff: purse. *In it*: several five-pound notes

LIGHTING PLOT

Property fittings required: *nil*

Interior. A hotel reception area and two bedrooms. The same scene throughout

ACT I

To open: General lighting in reception area and Green Room

Cue 1	**Roger** lies back down again to wait *Lights crossfade from Green Room to Blue Room*	(Page 3)
Cue 2	**Geoff** lies back on the bed to wait *Lights out in Blue Room*	(Page 5)
Cue 3	As **Ferris** goes out through the swing door *Lights up in the Green Room*	(Page 7)
Cue 4	**Roger** lies down *Lights out in Green Room*	(Page 10)
Cue 5	As **Ferris** goes out to the kitchen *Lights up in the Blue Room*	(Page 12)
Cue 6	**Geoff** lies down *Lights out in the Blue Room*	(Page 15)
Cue 7	As **Ferris** goes out through the swing door *Lights up in Green Room*	(Page 15)
Cue 8	As **Roger** goes out *Lights crossfade from Green Room to Blue Room*	(Page 15)
Cue 9	**Geoff** lies down again *Lights out in the Blue Room*	(Page 15)
Cue 10	As **Helen** and **Roger** go quickly out up opposite stairs *Lights up in Blue Room*	(Page 19)
Cue 11	**Geoff** goes to the telephone *Lights up in Green Room*	(Page 19)
Cue 12	As **Geoff** goes out, closing the door behind him *Lights out in Blue Room*	(Page 20)
Cue 13	As **Roger** stumbles out closing the door behind him *Lights out in Green Room*	(Page 21)
Cue 14	As **Ferris** goes out through the swing door *Lights up in Blue Room*	(Page 23)
Cue 15	**Geoff:** "You've still got your glasses on". *Lights crossfade from Blue Room to Green Room*	(Page 24)

| *Cue* 16 | **Roger** sits on the end of the bed | (Page 25) |
| | *Lights crossfade from Green Room to Blue Room* | |

| *Cue* 17 | As **Geoff** sips his champagne | (Page 27) |
| | *Lights out in Blue Room* | |

| *Cue* 18 | As **Ferris** goes up the R stairs | (Page 27) |
| | *Lights up in Green Room* | |

| *Cue* 19 | **Sally** sits on the low sofa | (Page 29) |
| | *Lights up in Blue Room* | |

| *Cue* 20 | **Geoff** goes out into the bathroom | (Page 33) |
| | *Lights out in Blue Room* | |

| *Cue* 21 | As **Ferris** starts to drink the Alka-Seltzer | (Page 33) |
| | *Black-out* | |

ACT II

To open: General lighting in Reception area and Green Room

| *Cue* 22 | **Roger** reacts and sits down beside **Helen** | (Page 35) |
| | *Lights out in Green Room* | |

| *Cue* 23 | As **Ferris** goes into the restaurant | (Page 36) |
| | *Lights up in Green Room* | |

| *Cue* 24 | **Roger** reacts | (Page 37) |
| | *Lights out in Green Room* | |

| *Cue* 25 | As **Ferris** goes back into the restaurant again | (Page 37) |
| | *Lights up in Green Room* | |

| *Cue* 26 | **Helen** goes into the bathroom | (Page 50) |
| | *Lights out in Green Room* | |

| *Cue* 27 | As **Ferris** and **Sally** go up the L stairs | (Page 50) |
| | *Lights up in Blue Room* | |

| *Cue* 28 | As **Ferris** starts to go out | (Page 51) |
| | *Lights out in Blue Room* | |

| *Cue* 29 | As **Sally** drags **Roger** into the restaurant | (Page 52) |
| | *Lights up in Green Room* | |

| *Cue* 30 | As **Helen** sits on the bed | (Page 53) |
| | *Lights out in Green Room* | |

| *Cue* 31 | As **Geoff** goes towards the R stairs | (Page 54) |
| | *Lights up in Green Room* | |

| *Cue* 32 | **Helen** and **Geoff** sit side-by-side | (Page 54) |
| | *Lights out in Green Room* | |

| *Cue* 33 | As **Ferris** goes towards the R stairs | (Page 55) |
| | *Lights up in Green Room* | |

| *Cue* 34 | As **Helen** and **Geoff** raise their glasses | (Page 56) |
| | *Lights crossfade from Green Room to Blue Room* | |

Cue 35	**Sally** pulls **Roger** on top of her *Lights out in Blue Room*	(Page 58)
Cue 36	As **Ferris** goes out through the swing door *Lights up in Green Room*	(Page 58)
Cue 37	**Geoff** sighs unhappily and sits down *Lights crossfade from Green Room to Blue Room*	(Page 58)
Cue 38	**Sally** and **Helen** react *Lights crossfade from Blue Room to Green Room*	(Page 61)
Cue 39	As **Roger** goes into the bathroom *Lights out in Green Room*	(Page 63)
Cue 40	As **Ferris** races off up the L stairs *Lights out in Blue Room*	(Page 63)
Cue 41	**Helen** sits on **Geoff**'s knee *Lights out in Blue Room*	(Page 65)
Cue 42	**Ferris** drags **Sally** off the R stairs *Lights up in Green Room*	(Page 65)
Cue 43	**Sally** and **Roger** look at each other *Lights out in Green Room*	(Page 67)
Cue 44	As **Ferris** races out up the L stairs *Lights up in Blue Room*	(Page 67)
Cue 45	**Helen** collects her chocolates and goes out *Lights out in Blue Room*	(Page 68)
Cue 46	As **Ferris** races off up R stairs *Lights up in Green Room*	(Page 69)
Cue 47	As **Ferris** goes out *Lights out in Green Room*	(Page 69)

EFFECTS PLOT
ACT I

Cue 1   *To open:*   (Page 1)
           Music, preferably "There's a Small Hotel", until dialogue begins

Cue 2   **Ferris:** "... nice of you to think of it, sir".   (Page 3)
           Music until dialogue begins

Cue 3   **Ferris:** "... nice of you to think of it, I'm sure."   (Page 5)
           Music until dialogue begins

Cue 4   Lights out in Green Room   (Page 10)
           Music until dialogue begins

Cue 5   **Roger** goes out up the R stairs   (Page 23)
           Music until dialogue begins

ACT II

Cue 9   As **Ferris** comes down the L stairs   (Page 52)
           Reception telephone rings

Cue 10   **Helen:** "Who did?"   (Page 59)
           Noise off stage from the bathroom

Cue 11   **Ferris:** "And don't start without me!"   (Page 73)
            Music swells